Ethics in the First Person

Ethics in the First Person

A Guide to Teaching and Learning Practical Ethics

Deni Elliott

ROWMAN & LITTLEFIELD PUBLISHERS, INC.
Lanham • Boulder • New York • Toronto • Oxford

ROWMAN & LITTLEFIELD PUBLISHERS, INC.

Published in the United States of America
by Rowman & Littlefield Publishers, Inc.
A wholly owned subsidiary of The Rowman & Littlefield Publishing Group, Inc.
4501 Forbes Boulevard, Suite 200, Lanham, Maryland 20706
www.rowmanlittlefield.com

PO Box 317
Oxford
OX2 9RU, UK

British Library Cataloguing in Publication Information Available

Library of Congress Cataloging-in-Publication Data

Elliott, Deni.
  Ethics in the first person : a guide to teaching and learning practical ethics /
Deni Elliott.
    p.   cm.
  Includes bibliographical references and index.
  ISBN-13: 978-0-7425-5206-7 (cloth : alk. paper)
  ISBN-10: 0-7425-5206-3 (cloth : alk. paper)
  ISBN-13: 978-0-7425-5207-4 (cloth : alk. paper)
  ISBN-10: 0-7425-5207-1 (cloth : alk. paper)
    1. Applied ethics—Study and teaching (Higher)   2. Moral education (Higher)
I. Title.
  BJ66.E45   2007
  170.71—dc22   2006004863

Printed in the United States of America

♾ ™ The paper used in this publication meets the minimum requirements of American
National Standard for Information Sciences—Permanence of Paper for Printed Library
Materials, ANSI/NISO Z39.48-1992.

This is dedicated with deep appreciation to my husband, Paul Martin Lester, who manages to be my best colleague and my best friend, and to my mother, Lottie Rhoads, who taught me how to do ethics in the first person.

Contents

Introduction

The problem with teaching and learning practical ethics is that the stories we tell are usually about *them*—other people who find themselves in the middle of some hard to imagine dilemma. They make wrong decisions, and the job of the reader is to figure out where the characters went wrong. For the most part, practical ethics literature focuses on people we do not want to meet in a dark alley.

The people who inhabit case studies are the scientists who fabricate data. Other cases focus on engineers and managers who decide that the number of lawsuits that will result from avoidable fatal car crashes costs the company less than replacing a problematic part or issuing a recall. Still others tell stories of the CEOs who trade on their insider knowledge and take no responsibility for the financial ruin of their employees, or stories of public officials who serve special interests instead of the public interest. The other people in practical ethics case scenarios are those who fall victims to these predators on society.

As long as case studies are morality tales that end with the recognition of the villains, their evil motives, and their harmful actions, there is little to recommend the study of practical ethics, except perhaps as a remedial course for the bad guys.

Practical ethics education needs to change its focus from fraud and fabrication to fluency and facilitation. The most interesting ethical problems occur when good people are trying hard to do the right thing. Decision making in the ethical sphere is woven throughout our everyday life, whether we ignore it or not. Unlike what we read in case studies, making a bad choice or a wrong decision in real life is the beginning of the adventure, not the end. For self-reflective people, making moral mistakes provides opportunity for growth and development.

It is essential, in learning ethics, to develop vocabulary so that we can talk better about the ethically relevant aspects of our decisions. Also essential is the interactive work that helps each teacher and student alike become more self-aware, self-reflective, and self-critical than each was before the start of class. In practical ethics classes, students and teachers should do the following:

1. Recognize our opportunities for moral decision making
2. Gain language to articulate our own values and beliefs, those of professions, and those of the communities in which we live
3. Open our eyes to the inconsistencies between what we say we believe and how we act
4. Feel safe enough to consider how we might act differently in the future

In short, teaching and learning practical ethics need to be first-person endeavors.

Over the past century, the movement in ethics education has been from theory to practice. It is ironic that this movement has been accompanied with a depersonalization of the practice. Philosophers of the classical past cared deeply about the experience, understanding, and action of the individual thinker. Aristotle tells us that the only good reason for studying ethics is to help us figure out how to become the best people we can be and how the experience of wise people around us can help in achieving that self-actualization.[1] Eighteenth-century German philosopher Immanuel Kant provides counsel for how each of us should reason through to the best action and how we ought to motivate ourselves to do morally required right actions.[2] Ethics, for these philosophers, was far more than an intellectual puzzle or a discussion of how some distant person or hypothetical character should act.

One way to reverse the trend of depersonalizing the practice of ethics is to recognize that it is essential to teach, learn, and practice practical ethics through the lens of first-person involvement. True ethics learning has taken place only when the individual learner perceives himself or herself as having changed. True ethics teaching takes place in a facilitative relationship between teacher and student in which both approach the subject material of human intention, choice, and conduct with the awe such powerful subject matter should provoke. Teacher and learner are changed through their work together when each teaching and learning interaction is recognized as carrying the potential for new moral growth for both. The subject matter of practical ethics is organic material for personal change in a way that few academic subjects can be.

Ethics in the First Person provides an opportunity for teachers of ethics to think more closely about their task. For instructors who choose to share the book with their students, it is an experiment in transparency for both students and teachers. It is also meant as a guide for those who are, on their own, looking for a systematic way to think about their own choices and actions. This is a book about our common quest to become fully developed human beings.

It rests on the foundation that if teachers and students can use what is happening in the ethics classroom as a basis for learning ethics, then the teaching and learning happen explicitly in the first person. This book also rests on the belief that the classroom is ethically rich, regardless of an instructor's willingness or unwillingness to make its content part of the discussion.

. *Ethics in the First Person* is the product of my experience—my experience as a graduate student of Sissela Bok at Harvard in the early 1980s, as an informal student of Daniel Callahan in my time as a member of a Hastings Center task force, and as an eager practitioner in the field of practical ethics since the late 1970s. This book is also the result of my attempt to bring to life the dream of Callahan, Bok, and other early thinkers of how teachers of practical ethics ought be taught.

Callahan rejects the notion that "only those with advanced degrees in moral philosophy or moral theology are properly qualified" to teach practical ethics. "It is ethics *and* law, ethics *and* biology, ethics *and* journalism [italics added], and so on."[3] The interdisciplinary nature of practical ethics teaching requires that the teacher of these courses have cross-disciplinary training. Callahan concludes that the adequate teacher of ethics is an "expert" in one field, such as journalism, law, business, or medicine, and a "competent amateur" in moral philosophy.[4] Or, if the person has expert-level training in moral philosophy, then being a competent amateur is required in the area of application. Callahan suggests that one could become a competent amateur through achieving mastery of the subject at the equivalent of a master's degree, which would take at least a year to achieve. The dream of developing such a program led me to leave my job as director of Dartmouth's Ethics Institute in 1992 to develop a graduate degree program in teaching ethics at the University of Montana.

The Master of Arts in Philosophy, Teaching Ethics Option, and its midcareer companion program, Advanced Graduate Studies in Teaching Ethics, was offered to students for the first time at the University of Montana in September 1997. With a three-year grant from the Fund for the Improvement of Postsecondary Education (Grant #P116B960045), these programs were designed to create the opportunity for graduate students, midcareer professors, and professionals to focus their study on one of the areas in which they needed to become competent amateurs so they could become adequate ethics educators: philosophical fundamentals or the related practical area. A core curriculum was devised to help participants weave moral philosophy and applied areas together. Eight years after the first class formed, more than three dozen students had completed their work or were actively enrolled. Some graduates have gone on to complete doctoral-level work in philosophy, education, journalism, or business. Other graduates took jobs teaching ethics in traditional and nontraditional settings. Along with those who are teaching in secondary or postsecondary education, graduates from the programs are involved in ethics education in the military, in medicine, in business, in sports, in journalism, and in government agencies. I'd like to think they are all striving for the ethical ideal in their own lives.

The programs have attracted a diverse group of talented students: high school and postsecondary teachers, educational administrators, physicians, nurses and allied health professionals, athletic trainers, military officers and lawyers, corporate executives, and traditional students who have recently completed undergraduate degrees in philosophy. Students have ranged in age from 22 to 65, with an almost equal mix of men and women. Some have entered the program with substantial publications, and others had not yet written an analytic paper.

As of fall 2001, all students were required to complete a core curriculum that included coursework in historical and contemporary moral theory, practical ethics, educational theory, and teaching ethics. In addition, students took courses and completed custom-designed practice teaching in their own particular areas of application. They created portfolios of their work and conducted primary research suitable for presentation and publication. Those lacking background in philosophy were required to take additional hours of coursework in philosophical history and logic.

As of this writing, the University of Montana's graduate programs in teaching ethics continue to welcome students with a variety of backgrounds, interests, and expertise. The rich variety of students' expertise results in a deeper and broader learning experience for all than could be attained with a more narrowly defined student body. Based on the extensive professional networking that has developed among the students, and the close friendships and romantic involvements as well, it is easy to note that the program has high social capital as well as educational significance. The programs have also attracted scholars and practitioners from around the world to the summer short courses in ethics offered through the Center for Ethics at the University of Montana.

As of fall 2005, I continue to teach in Montana's summer course program but now hold an endowed chair at the University of South Florida, St. Petersburg. I am grateful to the University of Montana for serving as my laboratory for teaching and research for so many productive years.

Ethics in the First Person is an accumulation of the work coming from my attempt to create the nation's laboratory school for teaching ethics, and it is offered with deep appreciation to the students in the teaching ethics programs from 1997 to 2003 who contributed to its development: Dean Anderson, Raquel Arouca, Wendy Barger, Jeff Cable, Samsara Chapman, Joslin Feinauer, Muriel Friedman, Brandt Geyerman, Debra Gorman-Bader, Frank Hale, Robert Hansen, James Harding, Glenn Hladek, Marion Hourdequin, William James, John Lee, Ivan Lorentzen, Andrew Meyer, Mike Monahan, Heidi Nunn, John Purdy, Dean Ritz, Peggy Shunick, Keith Shurtleff, Dan Sieckman, Logan Sisson, John Squillante, Jeffrey Stephenson, Matt Stockton, John Truslow, and Suzanne Wasilczuk.

This book is also offered with thanks to the Fund for the Improvement of Postsecondary Education, United States Department of Education, and program director Frank Frankfort for appreciating the vision and meaning of this experiment. Thanks also to Patrick McCormick and Colleen Hunter, program coordinators for the Practical Ethics Center, who sequentially nurtured the programs; and to assistants Regan Becker, Loren Meyer, and Justin Whitaker, who shared the vision; and to P. J. Balluck, who edited this manuscript. Thanks also to the University of South Florida, St. Petersburg, master's candidates Rita Florez, Heath Hooper, and Jeff Neely for converting the bibliography into standard form.

Last of all, thanks to the student, professional, and professorial participants in the Theory and Skills of Ethics Teaching summer seminar, 1998–2004, who helped shape this work by using it in its evolving manuscript stage.

Deni Elliott
June 2006

NOTES

1. See, for example, Aristotle, *Nicomachean Ethics*, Books 1–3, trans. Martin Ostwald (Upper Saddle River, NJ: Prentice Hall, 1999).

2. In Immanuel Kant, *Groundwork for a Metaphysics of Morals*, trans. H. J. Paton (New York: Harper, 1964).

3. Daniel Callahan and Sissela Bok, *Ethics Teaching in Higher Education* (New York: Hastings Center, 1980), 77.

4. Callahan and Bok, *Ethics Teaching*, 77.

Chapter One

Practical Ethics in Context

In 1980, the Hastings Center, an independent ethics research institute north of New York City, published a volume, *Teaching Ethics in Higher Education*, edited by Hastings Center cofounder Daniel Callahan and the center's codirector of their project on teaching ethics, Sissela Bok. That book, the first modern comprehensive treatment of practical ethics education, laid a conceptual foundation for the development and teaching of college courses. It focused on courses that were a departure from the traditional ethical theory taught in departments of philosophy and religion.

The book's publication followed a two-year project on the teaching of ethics in higher education that had produced nine monographs in higher education, law, journalism, bioethics, business, social sciences, engineering, policy, and undergraduate curriculum. Those monographs grew out of task forces, funded by the Rockefeller Brothers Fund and the Carnegie Corporation of New York, which conducted systematic descriptive studies of ethics teaching in these areas and provided normative guidance for how ethics should be taught.

The field of practical ethics grew steadily in the decades that followed. Professional societies were formed. Codes were written and revised. Academic standards for research were clarified if not completely articulated. Books in specialized ethics such as engineering, environment, forestry, government, journalism, law, medicine, military, and social work alone stacked up to thousands of titles. But if we are to understand the state of the field more than a quarter century after the publication of *Teaching Ethics in Higher Education*, we need also understand how the field developed prior to 1980. Indeed, Callahan points out that the agenda for the Hastings Center task forces developed in response to a perceived need for clarification of how and where ethics could be taught. "By the middle of the twentieth century, instruction in ethics had, by and large, become confined almost exclusively

7

to departments of philosophy and religion. Efforts to introduce ethics teaching in the professional schools and elsewhere in the university often met with indifference or outright hostility."[1]

The scholars who worked in practical ethics in the 1970s understood the struggle to create this new field. These researchers, students, and teachers rebelled against tradition and, often, against some of their own colleagues in the philosophy department, who thought of themselves as the only appropriate stewards of ethics teaching and scholarship. It was not easy to experiment with interdisciplinary ethics research or teaching or with work that bridged the expanse between the academy and professional practices. Qualified colleagues were few.

Today's students and scholars may not know the history and tradition that gave rise to the development of practical ethics as a field. They may not understand why some philosophers say that doing practical ethics does not count as *real* philosophy.[2] Those who have interest in specific areas, such as biomedical ethics, business ethics, engineering ethics, or scientific research ethics, may not understand the connection between classical philosophy and practical ethics. Professional ethics practice and teaching in some contexts have devolved into a single dictate: Learn and follow the code.

This chapter provides the context for current study and scholarship in the field. It is meant to explain the scope of practical ethics.

The Hastings Center's work in the late 1970s noted the beginning of a renewal of campus-wide and community-wide interest in ethics in situ. World War II, the development and use of atomic weapons, crises in leadership beginning with the Red Scare of the 1950s, and the Civil Rights movement all contributed to the defined need for public philosophy. As citizens and policy makers began talking explicitly about the ethical implications of their decisions, they looked for ethics experts. Some philosophers saw articles they were writing for philosophy journals being read by those grappling with real-life ethics issues in professional offices, in policy development, and in general public discussion.

It also became clear, during the 1970s, that philosophers were no longer the only scholars who could claim ethics expertise. Developmental psychologists such as William Perry, Lawrence Kohlberg, and Carol Gilligan were discussing ethics and how people might grow more morally sophisticated in their decision making. Practitioners and scholars trained in academic traditions other than in philosophy were developing codes of ethics and considering how vulnerable persons and populations should be treated by powerful societal institutions and professionals. A few universities were introducing education in ethical issues and analysis as part of the general education requirements for undergraduates, with the intent that students learn to think systematically through practical issues.[3]

A DEFINITION OF PRACTICAL ETHICS

The language used in the 1970s to describe the developing field of practical ethics reflected the varied background of the practitioners engaged in that work. Philosophers called the field *applied ethics*. They perceived the practical work in ethics as application of classical philosophical theories and methodologies to real-life problems. Professionals who were engaged in developing codes and normative principles for specific professions such as engineering, medicine, and journalism called the field *professional ethics*.

Here, I use the term *practical ethics*, which evolved through the late twentieth century to become an umbrella term used by researchers, teachers, and practitioners, regardless of their original discipline and training. Practical ethics, while somewhat redundant,[4] does not imply that a particular classical philosophical theory will provide the single correct answer to a contemporary practical problem, nor does it confine its focus to an identified profession.

Practical ethics is used to indicate a cluster of activities that, in any particular situation, includes at least some of the following:

- Study of the ways that people act within particular roles or occupations
- Study of the ways that professions and social institutions connect with one another and of how well societal roles or needs are met through the complementary nature of social institutions and professions
- Creation and analysis of codes of ethics or other professional or role-related standards of behavior
- Analysis of past, present, or possible actions of moral agents, leading to normative judgments of what they should or should not do
- Analysis of concepts, such as truth telling, confidentiality, consent, and privacy, as well as analysis of role-related responsibilities
- Analysis of morally questionable behaviors, such as being the cause of physical or emotional harm, deception, promise breaking, neglect of duty, and lawbreaking, to determine if these acts are morally permitted or prohibited in particular cases
- Analysis of differences and similarities between the normative assumptions that sustain cultural, professional, and social groups

The tools needed to carry out this array of tasks come from a variety of academic disciplines.

The *descriptive* activity of studying and detailing what individuals, groups, or social institutions actually *do*, and *why* they do certain things, uses clinical, ethnographic, historical, qualitative, and quantitative methodologies. Descriptive scholarship also includes in-depth inquiry into the aspects of particular cases—Who did what and why? What chain of events or chain of reasoning led to a particular action or conclusion? Descriptive scholarship includes collecting data regarding individuals' perceptions about moral permissibility and how people report how they and others behave. It includes content analyses—examining people pictured in advertisements, for example, and noting the stories that the visual content tells us about those pictured. Teachings from anthropology, history, journalism, political science, psychology, and sociology all assist the researcher in completing descriptive ethics inquiry.

Philosophical methodology provides the reasoning tools for determining what is an ethical issue and why. Philosophy provides processes for determining which activities are morally required, permitted, prohibited, or encouraged. The researcher uses philosophical tools to explore whether certain acts *should* count as examples of right or wrong intent or action. Philosophical methodology allows the researcher to define and describe morally relevant aspects such as moral agency, accountability, and those affected by action.

Philosophical argument is ultimately used to justify particular choices. But while conceptualization and justification are philosophical activities, theory alone will not provide answers for problems in practical ethics.[5]

Thus, practical ethics, as studied and practiced in the twenty-first century, is truly an "interdiscipline" that depends on literature and methodologies from an array of scholarly disciplines and traditions. It is also multifaceted in that work in practical ethics relies on the experience and role expectations of the individual, profession, or social institution under study.

THE EVOLUTION OF PRACTICAL ETHICS

In many ways, today's practical ethics is a revival of philosophy in its earliest Western expression. The Greek philosopher Socrates, heralded as the founder of Western philosophy, engaged in his work between 500 and 450 BCE. We know from the writings of Plato, a student of Socrates, that Socrates took his philosophical discussions to the streets of Athens.[6] His philosophical analysis, whether in moral philosophy, metaphysics, or logic, invited all others brave enough to use Socrates' method of thinking out loud and following assertions to their logical and often comical implications. This important, thoughtful analysis was considered to be the right, if not the duty, of every citizen. The job of the philosopher was to facilitate thought and discussion among citizens. Moral reasoning was understood to be too important to isolate in the academy and too human not to be ironic, pragmatic, and funny.

Moral philosophy, the study of ethics, evolved into a scholarly pursuit in the early twentieth century that barely resembled either the work of Socrates or of contemporary practical ethics.

Picking a starting point from which to describe the development of practical ethics as a contemporary field is an exercise in chronological randomness. I choose the beginning of the twentieth century because that time marks a major shift in emphasis within higher education as a whole and within the study of philosophy. These shifts, and the intellectual paradigm within which the shifts occurred, helped create the foundations from which the study of practical ethics developed.

At the turn of the twentieth century, administrators in institutions of higher education were changing their view of their role from moral guide, which focused on the development of student character, to objective dispenser of truth, with focus on description of external reality. This change is well illustrated by the Amherst College example cited by Sloan.

> In 1895, the Amherst College catalogue devoted the entire first page of the section on "The Course of Study" to a description of the course in ethics taught by the president of the college to the senior class. But by 1905 ethics had disappeared from its front-page billing in the catalogue, and was to be found as merely one among several courses offered in Amherst's philosophy department as an elective for sophomores.[7]

This shift, from the university as moral teacher to the university as developer and dispenser of value-free knowledge, is the complicated result of many changes in American life. At the turn of the twentieth century, the sciences created, and then reflected, a naïve public assumption that humankind could use empirical tools and human invention to unlock the secrets of all that existed. The focus of higher education in the early twentieth century was the development of the students' powers of observation and analysis so that the truths of the outside world would be uncovered in the process.

Just as general education had turned its focus from individual growth to discoveries of external reality, a trend in moral philosophy turned the study of ethics away from individual decision making. Many American moral philosophers in the early twentieth century based their work on that of the British philosopher G. E. Moore. Moore delineated the project for ethics as one that was primarily linguistic in nature. Moore's concern was the meaning of *good*. He criticized earlier work in moral philosophy on the basis that philosophers equated "goodness" with naturalist words such as *happiness, pleasure,* or *utility.* By "naturalist," Moore meant that these concepts were products of human experience and thus subjective rather than objectively true. Moore said it was a mistake to see "goodness" as synonymous with these human-experience-centered terms, and he dubbed this the "naturalistic fallacy." Moore determined that all work in ethics that was based on equating "goodness" with some human attribute was flawed at its foundation.[8]

American philosophers, such as R. B. Perry, E. Nagel, S. Hook, and C. I. Lewis, took up the challenge of G. E. Moore. They attempted to find objective knowledge of good and evil, right and wrong, which was not dependent on qualities of human experience.[9] These philosophers defined the role of philosophy to be the strict analysis of a statement's meaning.

Of course, not all philosophers of that time were content to theorize separate from practice. The American pragmatist philosophers, Charles Sanders Peirce, William James, George Herbert Mead, and John Dewey, for example, attempted to unify the human endeavors of theorizing with practical life. According to Israel Scheffler,

> [P]ragmatism does not reduce or subordinate philosophical and other human interests to a simplified model of positive science. In the first place, it is the theory of evolution and the new statistical modes of reasoning that have exercised the greatest impact upon pragmatism, and that have led it to criticize inherited conceptions of science itself. In the second place, pragmatism takes quite seriously the legitimate demands of other modes of human experience—morality and social practice; art, poetry, history; religion and philosophical speculation. It does not use *de facto* science as a device for excluding or downgrading these other modes. Rather, it takes science as suggestive of more general concepts of critical thought, in terms of which the continuities among all modes may be revealed, and in light of which they may all be refined and advanced.[10]

Unlike their positivist brethren, pragmatists sought to integrate logical method with experience, to link abstract ideas with common sense. While the pragmatists produced important works at the turn of the twentieth century and into the 1930s, the importance of their work was ultimately overshadowed in philosophical circles by the positivists. The positivists also worked toward the development of unified theory but kept their analysis at an abstract level. Scheffler remarks,

> The mediating or unifying cast of pragmatism has not been much in evidence in post-Deweyian philosophy in America. As Morton White remarks, "after Dewey, American philosophy entered a new phase in which it altered its conception of its responsibilities." In this phase, philosophers gave their primary attention to epistemological and semantic questions. Such concerns put them "at the opposite end of

the spectrum from pundits and sages who immerse themselves so deeply in the spiritual issues of their time that they make hardly any effort to reason systematically."[11]

According to contemporary moral philosopher Bernard Rosen, "Teachers who attempted to raise actual moral problems to normative theories were often regarded as preachers, and as not engaged in their proper profession. And even when normative ethical theories were discussed, it was in regard to their claims about meta-ethical concerns."[12]

World War II marks the start of events that shook some moral philosophers from their "ivory tower" theorizing. That war illustrated the capability of humans to intentionally cause enormous evil to other humans outside of direct combat. While human cruelty toward others was not new, this was the first war fought within the context of continuous media feed. Through radio broadcasts from various "fronts" and wire transmissions of stories and pictures, evil, for the first time, had a real-time global audience.

The world's citizens struggled to understand. Psychologists and educators looked for social causes to explain Hitler and the willingness of German citizens to go along with the mass execution of innocent people. The psychology of kamikaze pilots, an early version of suicide bombers, defied comprehension. Teachings from the field of moral philosophy, along with understandings from psychology, sociology, anthropology, and political science, were dissected with the naïve belief that understanding could prevent atrocities from happening again.

Soon after the war, U.S. citizens and policy makers in the United States became fearful of the threat of other political ideologies, Communism in particular. The U.S. Senate conducted hearings on supposed un-American activities, accusing citizens of being Communists and demanding that they inform on their friends. Moral philosophers found it timely to consider what citizens owed the state and what they did not; they brought their theoretical knowledge and philosophical history to the present-day question of legitimate limits of state power. Much of U.S. policy and law had been founded on the celebration of the individual. McCarthyism provided a sobering reminder that nineteenth-century British philosopher John Stuart Mill was right in suggesting that doctrine assumed to be true becomes dogma difficult to overturn.[13]

The Civil Rights movement provided opportunities for philosophical analysis in addition to the legal analysis already taking place. Civil disobedience and questions of justification for the use of violence by protestors and by authorities required the application of ethical thought.

The unpopular Vietnam War found philosophers, politicians, and citizens learning about and then debating just war theory.

The social issues of the 1970s inspired more philosophical input: the newly articulated rights of women, people of non-Anglo backgrounds, people with disabilities, and other groups that were not politically dominant; abortion; and questions regarding the responsibility of the state toward individuals attracted a new generation of philosophers who were willing to share their ideas with the nonphilosophers who wanted to resolve social problems.

Technological advances in medicine created new questions of fairness, such as who, among various candidates, should receive a transplant or access to a single dialysis machine. Technology also created new moral questions brought into being by the possibilities offered by technology. What counts as death? What counts as life? Do pregnant women have a responsibility to access information regarding the health of their developing fetuses? Is the destruction of preimplantation embryos morally equivalent to abortion?

Watergate and other scandals diminished citizens' trust in the authority of social institutions and created a forum for discussion of the role-related responsibilities of politicians, professionals, and others in power. Just as philosophers were finding that others had interest in how to reason through these questions, citizens were less willing to accept the assumption that those in power were necessarily operating out of a theory of social benefit.

Today, some philosophers remain adamant that their efforts to elaborate ethical theories and clarify the meaning of moral terms do not make them specialists in dealing with practical normative questions. However, other philosophers and nonphilosophers with education and expertise in practical ethics believe they have what philosopher Tim Dare calls *ethical expertise*:

> Ethical expertise will require a certain body of knowledge: knowledge of philosophical problems, questions, positions, and theories (e.g., ethical theories, theories of knowledge, views about human nature and society), knowledge of the assumptions, consequences, and criticisms of different positions or views, knowledge of types of arguments, and likely problems (e.g., fallacies like false dichotomy or ambiguity of scope). Ethical expertise will require commitment to certain values associated with good reasoning, such as commitment to understanding issues and views, commitment to reasoned support and evaluation of beliefs or claims, willingness to question key assumptions and challenge received wisdom, and interest in finding solutions to philosophical questions and problems.[14]

The term *ethicist*, so common in discussions of practical ethics in the twenty-first century, did not appear in print prior to the 1970s. Indeed, the Callahan/Bok book provides an early use of the term in scholarly forum.[15] *Ethicist* seems to have developed from journalists' need to describe their sources in concise ways. The news stories on the important social issues of the day required someone with expertise to explain, for the lay audience, just how to comprehend the problem at hand. Reporters turned to philosophers who were working and publishing on practical ethics concerns. *Ethicist* was used by news organizations because it was shorter than describing the news source as someone "who teaches ethics" or someone who is a "philosopher with interest in relevant ethical issues." For the layperson and journalist alike, *ethicist* is less ambiguous than the label *moral philosopher*, which may be construed to describe the character of the person rather than her field of study. *Ethicist* has come to be used to describe someone with "ethical expertise."[16]

It is not surprising that pragmatism is once again emerging as an important philosophical trend in the study of practical ethics. Contemporary philosopher Richard Gilmore connects contemporary neopragmatism with the pragmatism of the early 1900s with the teleology of Aristotle. Says Gilmore,

> To take up the question of teleology is to take up the question of what is the function of a human being and how he or she can best fulfill it. Stated in this way, and this formulation is, I think, consistent with Aristotle's formulation of the question. I would have to agree with [Richard] Rorty, [Cornell] West, [Richard] Bernstein, et al, that the question is fundamentally, and in principle, unanswerable. However, if the question is asked in a slightly different way, that is, if it is asked without the presumption of some meta-function, but rather is asked from within the context of being human and having human needs, desires, and limitations (which is also consistent with Aristotle), if the question is asked in the form of, for example, "Is there something I can do that can contribute to my leading the best life that I can possibly lead?" with "best" here referring to an idea of an overall maximized satisfaction with my life, then the question is answerable, and it is worth the time of our life to try to answer it. This formulation of the question has a strongly instrumentalist tone, which is consistent with pragmatism, new and old, but it also contains the suggestion of an objective, non-relative telios, the "best" life I can live.[17]

There have been important changes in the development of practical ethics since the noted new beginning in the 1970s. A review of twelve generalizations by the Hastings Center in the late 1970s shows how practical ethics has grown since then.

1. *Most courses and programs outside traditional departments are financed by external short-term grants rather than by general university funds or state appropriations.*[18]

Twenty-five years after that observation, ethics courses are thriving outside of philosophy departments with full state funding, as are interdisciplinary programs that combine philosophy and science, or philosophy and law, for example. These courses serve undergraduate, graduate, and professional students. A look at the Association for Practical and Professional Ethics (APPE) website provides an impressive sampling.[19]

As of spring 2005, twenty-three schools list graduate degrees in some area of practical ethics on the APPE website.[20] The Center for Environmental Philosophy lists an additional thirteen schools that have graduate programs in environmental ethics.[21] Many of these institutions also offer postbaccalaureate certificate programs. Ten other schools on the APPE website note undergraduate or graduate certificate programs as well.

Some schools require that all undergraduates take coursework that links classical moral philosophy with contemporary moral practice.

2. *Most programs in applied ethics have been initiated within the past ten years.*[22]

That statement was certainly true in 1980; but since 1980, programs, courses, professional organizations, and centers have multiplied. The centers, programs, and professional organizations that are institutional members of the Association for Practical and Professional Ethics total 117, as of the February 2005 directory. Only 4 of these—Center for Business Ethics at Bentley College; Center for Professional Ethics at Case Western Reserve University; Poynter Center for the Study of Ethics and American Institutions at Indiana University; and the Division of Technology, Culture, and Communication at the University of Virginia—list a founding date prior to 1980.

3. *Most ethics and "values" courses are elective rather than required.*[23]

An increasing number of accreditation councils now require preprofessional training in ethics. The United States Public Health Service requires that investigators and graduate students funded through their grant programs receive training in ethics and in the proper use of human participants in research. The Animal Welfare Act requires that researchers who use animals have ethics training. While the number of universities that require ethics as part of general undergraduate education are relatively few, the trend toward requiring ethics training as part of preprofessional or professional majors is increasing.

4. *Most such courses are interdisciplinary in content; many are team-taught and not confined to departments of religion or philosophy.*[24]

Team-taught courses are less in favor now than they were in the 1970s. Team-taught courses are expensive to teach as they require double instructors. Competent teachers of practical ethics are now more readily available. Many practitioners and educators who lack doctoral-level degrees in philosophy have developed their philosophical expertise in other ways. Philosophers who teach practical ethics courses have developed expertise in one or more areas of specialization.

It certainly is less confusing for students if they are taught by one professor who can integrate philosophical process with an area of specialization than to be taught by two professors who may not even share a common language for ethics discussions. The team approach often presented moral philosophy as distinct from the ethical issues and then left it up to the students to create bridges between the two. As the professors teaching the course often did not model how the bridging was possible, it is easy to see that students might be confused about how to link the two.

> 5. *Most use the case-method approach in conjunction with other forms of pedagogy, such as the services of visiting lecturers and continuing seminars.*[25]

Case method is still a prevalent teaching method in practical ethics. Many of the published textbooks in the field are filled with real or hypothetical cases, some as short as a paragraph; others are book length. Case method, as it developed out of law-school teaching, has the goal of teaching students how to recognize principles and precedent from case material. The case method that is generally used in teaching practical ethics tends to be more free-ranging and less focused on recognizing precedent.

As the appreciation of high-quality scholarship in practical ethics has grown, the tendency to use the services of experienced practitioners to "teach" in the field has diminished. Hearing war stories of longtime practitioners and having an opportunity to interact with those making the tough decisions will always be important for preprofessional students. But hearing morality tales from the field is now understood as different from learning ethics.

> 6. *Most courses are issue oriented (e.g., dealing with euthanasia, bribery, atomic power) rather than organized around a very broad ethical theme (e.g., justice, individualism).*[26]

Whether a course today focuses on issues rather than on broad ethical themes depends on the purpose of the course. Courses can be created around broad ethical themes or around specific issues. A course in ethics and public affairs, for example, is likely to take on the tension between individual and community, merit versus need, and similar broad ethical themes. A course in nursing ethics is more likely to focus on the role-related responsibilities of individual practitioners. Instructors who bring background and expertise in political science, economics, or sociology are likely to look at the broad picture that includes the introduction of themes. Instructors who come from a professional background may focus on individual practitioner issues or even limit the course to those issues raised within the profession's code of ethics.

In addition, the development of ethics within areas of specialization seems to have moved from a focus on the individual practitioner and the ethical problems he might encounter to a broader look at how the institution or profession should operate within a societal context. Today, ethics courses are likely to address "macro" issues—the role that the practice or profession plays in society—as well as the micro issues that practitioners confront.

7. *The impetus for the inauguration of special ethics programs comes from many sources, including students, faculty, administration, and professional societies.*[27]

Today, courses and programs have become a stable part of institutions of higher education because of recognized need and a market for the courses. Now, ethics teaching is a specialty or subspecialty of faculty from a variety of disciplines.[28] Another recent factor that has influenced practical ethics teaching has been donors who are particularly interested in supporting teaching or research in the field. Fellows programs, such as the Laurence S. Rockefeller Visiting Fellowships at Princeton University, and full centers, such as the Markkula Center for Applied Ethics at Santa Clara University, have provided opportunities for growth in the field that would have been unlikely without external support.

8. *An increasing number of courses and programs on ethics are aimed explicitly at preprofessional students.*[29]

While it is true that professional societies, accrediting agencies, and preprofessional curricula committees have recognized the need to include explicit ethics teaching as preparation for particular practice, the field is much broader than mere introduction of preprofessionals to the value questions they will confront in the future.

Environmental ethics is a good example of a subarea of practical ethics that has developed without a particular professional constituency in mind. Arguments from environmental ethics conclude that humankind, as a whole, has responsibilities to animals and to biosystems, not just those people whose special role-related responsibilities include stewardship of land, water, and air quality. In spring 2005, the Center for Environmental Philosophy listed twenty-one schools that either offered graduate degree study in environmental ethics or that had related graduate programs.[30] Amazon.com lists 741 books in "environmental ethics."[31] Cross-cultural courses in Eastern or indigenous ethics span human perspective without reference to particular career choices. Indeed, many "professional" ethics courses, such as those in journalism or medical ethics, provide content that empowers consumers as well as prepares future practitioners.

Some schools have included service-learning experiences in attempts to promote the development of character or the learning of ethics.[32]

9. *Ethics programs do not usually constitute student majors but complement them.*[33]

As discussed previously, graduate programs with majors in practical ethics have been offered to students since the 1990s. Undergraduate programs have been slower to adopt full majors, but interdisciplinary minor or certificate programs are easy to find. For example, John Wesley College advertises a major in management and ethics, and Union University advertises a major in Christian ethics. Oregon State University, the University of Georgia, and York University in Toronto all advertise interdisciplinary certificate programs in practical ethics.[34]

10. *Comparatively more ethics courses and programs at the undergraduate level have been instituted at schools that now have, or had, religious or denominational ties than is the case at public institutions.*[35]

Public institutions in the 1980s and 1990s developed secular-based programs and coursework in practical ethics. As the focus in practical ethics in those decades was analytic thought and moral reasoning skills, no religious tradition was necessary to justify the courses to skeptical colleagues or curriculum committees. The courses were seen to be direct offshoots of traditional moral philosophy and often developed out of departments of philosophy rather than of religion.

11. *Some disciplinary friction exists concerning who is qualified to teach ethics and in what manner ethics should be taught.*[36]

Callahan points out that the interdisciplinary nature of practical ethics requires an interdisciplinary background on the part of the professor.

A person trained exclusively in ethics will not be fully qualified to teach such courses; other knowledge will have to be acquired. Yet, by the same token, someone trained in a discipline other than ethics can become qualified to teach ethics, if, in addition to training in his or her own field, he or she acquires the necessary ethical training. . . . A traditional distinction should make the point perfectly clear: when the teaching of ethics requires the knowledge of two or more fields, it is a necessary but not sufficient condition that there be a full grounding in one of the fields; a sufficient condition will be some degree of grounding in the other field as well.[37]

Interdisciplinary preparation for instructors became a cottage industry in the latter two decades of the twentieth century. Short courses, usually presented as five-day workshops in teaching ethics in particular fields, such as engineering, health care, and journalism, attracted hundreds of educators and helped them begin to fill in the gaps in their backgrounds. More year-long programs need to be developed to help adequately prepare ethics teachers in response to Callahan's and Bok's summary recommendations:

An advanced degree in philosophy or religion is the minimal standard for ethics courses taught within the disciplinary perspectives of those fields. As an ideal, those teaching applied and professional ethics—where knowledge of one or more fields is necessary—ought to have the equivalent of one year of training in the field in which they were not initially trained. . . . Training programs of two kinds are needed: first, programs to assist those with no training in ethics to gain a basic knowledge of that field, and, second, programs for those trained in ethics that will allow them to work for the equivalent of a year in another field.[38]

12. *Many of the new "core curriculum" programs now under way or in the process of development give a prominent place to ethical and "value" issues; yet in few places has that general commitment given rise to systematic programs.*[39]

Systematic programs have developed with the clear consensus among schools offering undergraduate programs and those offering graduate programs in practical ethics that significant preparation in classical moral philosophy is necessary for students to develop the ability to theorize and apply logical tools to their analysis of moral problems. However, students with no philosophical training may be successful in a practical ethics course that acquaints them with general issues or professional expectations. But they may not be equipped to fully utilize philosophical method in analyzing cases or may not develop a full understanding of philosophical concepts.

One major change that has developed in practical ethics teaching and research over the last two decades of the twentieth century is an understanding that practical ethics needs a bigger toolkit than one provided by classical Western moral philosophy. At a minimum, the specific practices or professions being analyzed require tools for analysis that take into account the unique context of that practice or profession.

The trick has been to figure out how to integrate the best tools from philosophy and practice while leaving room for yet other tools. According to Dare,

> One reason to try to hold onto [Western moral philosophical] theory is that effective criticism seems at least occasionally to require us to step outside the particular practices of the communities with which we are concerned, to have recourse to general standards or principles of evaluation.[40]

But, Dare asserts, theories and principles cannot provide the total answer. "They are tools in moral reasoning rather than self-contained machines for the generation of moral answers."[41]

Feminist critique of Western moral philosophy, postmodern rejections of the enlightenment traditions, and the additions of Eastern and indigenous approaches to ethical theory have all provided the researcher in practical ethics with a variety of tools and the clear challenge to justify the use of specific tools in specific situations.

According to ethics scholar Earl Winkler,

> In place of the traditional, essentially top-down model of moral reasoning and justification, contextualism adopts the general idea that moral problems must be resolved within the interpretive complexities of concrete circumstances, by appeal to relevant historical and cultural traditions, with reference to critical institutional and professional norms and virtues, and by relying primarily upon the method of comparative case analysis. According to this method we navigate our way to a practical resolution by discursive triangulation from clear and settled cases to problematic ones.[42]

The goal of practical ethics study and scholarship at the turn of the twenty-first century can perhaps still best be described by a philosopher from the early twentieth century. That's not surprising. One of the basic understandings of the philosophical tradition is that philosophers often speak to one another across the ages. True philosophical wisdom is not time-bound or culture-bound. According to Morton White, as quoted in Scheffler,

> In the middle of the spectrum . . . between highly specialized epistemologists and great-souled sages, there are philosophers who have their epistemologies all right, but who keep them warm by linking them to reflections on the great disciplines and institutions of civilization. They try to discourse intelligibly on the nature of mathematics, natural science, metaphysics, morals, history, art, law, politics, education, or religion; they advance views on man's condition and his fate; they offer analyses and assessments of their times; they are technicians but not mere technicians; they are seers but not madmen.[43]

Scholars with ethical expertise are increasingly finding professional homes in corporations, medical centers, and governmental and nonprofit agencies, as well as in institutions of higher education. Citizens all, we are recognizing again that we have the right, if not the duty, to think and act on the important issues of the day.

NOTES

1. Daniel Callahan, "Foreword," in *Ethics in the Undergraduate Curriculum*, ed. Bernard Rosen and Arthur L. Caplan (New York: Hastings Center, 1980), v.

2. This is what I was told by some philosophy professors and graduate students who were studying a more traditional curriculum when I was doing my graduate work in philosophy at Wayne State University and Harvard. To my surprise, despite having spent most of my academic career as a professor of philosophy, I hear the same criticisms echoed by young philosopher colleagues more than twenty-five years later.

3. Douglas Sloan, "The Teaching of Ethics in the American Undergraduate Curriculum, 1876–1976," in *Ethics Teaching in Higher Education*, ed. Daniel Callahan and Sissela Bok (New York: Plenum, 1980), 1–57.

4. Who would want to study "impractical" ethics?

5. Philosophy also gives us the possibly distracting use of *moral* and *ethical* as synonyms.

6. Ancient Greeks were known by one name and differentiated by their birth city. Socrates was "Socrates of Athens," Plato was "Plato of Athens," and Aristotle was "Aristotle of Stagira."

7. Sloan, "Teaching of Ethics," 9.

8. Sloan, "Teaching of Ethics," 34.

9. A distinction should be noted between these twentieth-century American philosophers and the eighteenth-century German philosopher Immanuel Kant. Like these later philosophers, Kant argued that human experience was neither a necessary nor sufficient condition for determining that something is morally "good." However, unlike American positivist philosophers, Kant believed that the purpose of the study of ethics was to determine right action for actual human beings. So while Kant believed that moral theory could be constructed out of a rational base alone, the goal was for people to figure out how to act in morally correct ways.

10. Israel Scheffler, *Four Pragmatists: A Critical Introduction to Peirce, James, Mead, and Dewey* (New York: Humanities, 1974), 2.

11. Scheffler, *Four Pragmatists*, 2–3.

12. Bernard Rosen, "The Teaching of Undergraduate Ethics," in *Ethics Teaching in Higher Education*, ed. Daniel Callahan and Sissela Bok (New York: Plenum, 1980), 176.

13. John Stuart Mill, "On Liberty," in *On Liberty and Other Essays*, ed. John Gray (New York: Oxford University Press, 1991), 48–49.

14. Tim Dare, "Challenges to Applied Ethics," in *Encyclopedia of Applied Ethics*, ed. Daniel Callahan and Peter Singer (New York: Academic, 1998), 186.

15. See, for example, Sloan, "Teaching of Ethics," 56.

16. However, I, like some people who teach and research in practical ethics, dislike the term *ethicist* because of the common misunderstanding that such a person provides the ethically correct answer.

17. Richard Gilmore, "Pragmatism, Perfectionism, and Feminism," www.bu.edu/wcp/Papers/Gend/GendGilm.htm (accessed February 10, 2003).

18. Hastings Center, *The Teaching of Ethics in Higher Education: A Report by the Hastings Center* (New York: Hastings Center, 1980), 22.

19. Association for Practical and Professional Ethics, php.ucs.indiana.edu/~appe/study.html (accessed April 17, 2005).

20. Association for Practical and Professional Ethics, "Study Opportunities in Practical and Professional Ethics," www.indiana.edu/~appe/study.html (accessed April 17, 2005).

21. Center for Environmental Philosophy, "Environmental Ethics Graduate Programs," www.cep.unt.edu/other.html (accessed April 17, 2005).

22. Hastings Center, *Teaching of Ethics*, 22.

23. Hastings Center, *Teaching of Ethics*, 22.

24. Hastings Center, *Teaching of Ethics*, 22.

25. Hastings Center, *Teaching of Ethics*, 22.

26. Hastings Center, *Teaching of Ethics*, 22.

27. Hastings Center, *Teaching of Ethics*, 22.

28. At the University of Montana, for example, in a campus-wide survey in 2003, 10 percent of full-time faculty identified ethics as a major teaching or research area.

29. Hastings Center, *Teaching of Ethics*, 22.

30. Center for Environmental Philosophy, "Graduate Programs," www.cep.unt.edu/other.html.

31. Amazon.com, www.amazon.com/exec/obidos (accessed April 17, 2005).

32. Please see chapter 3 for more complete treatment of the topic of service learning.

33. Hastings Center, *Teaching of Ethics*, 22.

34. Association for Practical and Professional Ethics, "Study Opportunities," www.indiana.edu/~appe/study.html.

35. Hastings Center, *Teaching of Ethics*, 23.

36. Hastings Center, *Teaching of Ethics*, 23.

37. Daniel Callahan, "Qualifications for the Teaching of Ethics," in *Ethics Teaching in Higher Education*, ed. Daniel Callahan and Sissela Bok (New York: Plenum, 1980), 77.

38. Callahan, "Qualifications," 80.

39. Hastings Center, *Teaching of Ethics*, 22–23.

40. Dare, "Challenges to Applied Ethics," 187.

41. Dare, "Challenges to Applied Ethics," 188.

42. Earl Winkler, "Encyclopedia of Applied Ethics," ed. Ruth Chadwick, Dan Callahan, and Peter Singer (London: Academic Press, 1997), 194–195.

43. Morton White, *Science and Sentiment in America* (New York: Oxford University Press, 1972), quoted in Scheffler, *Four Pragmatists*, 3.

Chapter Two

Teaching and Learning Ethics in an Ethical Environment

Ethics cannot be divorced from context. In class, we might discuss the ethics of journalists or nurses or other professionals, but the intellectually curious student and teacher will consider the application of that learning to the situation closest to hand, the ethics classroom.

Greg Johnson, the business ethics teacher who stars in the following case, is a composite of the eager, young assistant professors who have attended the Theory and Skills of Ethics Teaching seminar that I have taught for many summers at the University of Montana.

The case developed from the embarrassing moments that I and others have shared in that seminar about what happens when students expect their instructors to practice as well as preach ethical standards.

Greg Johnson, assistant professor of management, had long decided that the business ethics course was his favorite. He often found ways to discuss ethics in his other management courses, but he found it most stimulating to have students spend a semester with no goal more important than honing their ability to recognize and think through important ethical issues.

The first few semesters that he taught the course, he worried about the mix of students. The class was required for upper-level undergraduate majors, many of whom had never seen the inside of a corporation, and for MBA candidates, most of whom returned to school with significant management experience. The class was offered as one large section, accommodating about eighty students each year. Now, three years into teaching the course, Greg found that the idealism of the undergraduates contrasted nicely with the cynicism of the graduate students. Greg knew that he leaned toward a socially responsible imperative for business, so he thought it was good for the under-

graduates to hear the strong bottom-line philosophy that many of the return-
ing students brought. And he thought it was good for those MBA candidates
to defend their belief that the basic job of business was to please its stock-
holders.

Greg was careful to tell students early in the term that it was not his job
to teach them what to think. Rather his job was to introduce them to some
issues that they needed to think about and to teach them some defensible
processes for thinking through those issues. He told the students that he
would not hide his own reasoned conclusions, and he encouraged students to
make him defend his beliefs. He wanted his own process of reasoning to be
transparent and defensible. He wanted to model good ethical analysis for the
students. Students were free to reach their own conclusions, different from
his, with the understanding that they, too, would be asked to present well-
reasoned arguments for their claims.

Greg believed he was a good ethics teacher. But now, almost halfway
through the current term, he felt as if he was losing control of the class.

The problem started three weeks into the term. Generally, everything had
been going well. Students he called on had read the assigned case and were
pretty much on target in identifying basic issues. The undergraduates didn't
seem intimidated, and the MBA candidates were eager to share their experi-
ence. Greg often heard students talking about the case as they left the room
at the end of class.

In summing up this particular class, Greg thought he had made a noncon-
troversial observation about corporate life: "Corporations that are con-
cerned about ethics give employees power and voice to make change in the
organization."

Greg remembered closing his book at the end of the sentence, signaling
the end of class. At that moment, Steven, a candidate in the MBA program
who had five years of management experience, asked from the back of the
room, "Does that hold for classrooms too? How about for the university as
a whole? Are student voices necessary to make this organization ethical?"

Greg responded off the top of his head. "Ethics in higher education is dif-
ferent from ethics in corporate life," he chuckled. "That would be a whole
semester's course of its own. But obviously, in this class, student voices are
necessary to make the case method work."

The next week, John, another MBA candidate, pushed the corporation-
classroom analogy. The case concerned employee evaluation. Greg summa-
rized one of the points the students had discussed: "An ethical performance
evaluation is based on clear and public criteria, known to the employee well
in advance." John's hand shot up. Greg nodded in his direction, and John
said, "Will you please distribute the midterm exam questions to us?"

The request was so unexpected and unconnected to the conversation that Greg just shook his head in bewilderment. "Excuse me?"

"Well," John said, "you just gave us the rule for deciding if an evaluation is ethical. Doesn't it follow that you should give us the exam questions well ahead of time so that we have public knowledge of the criteria upon which we are being evaluated?"

"This is a classroom, not a corporation," Greg responded. "You are students, not staff dealing with employment at will."

By the following week, the undergraduates had picked up on the graduate students' lead even if they didn't relate the questions to the business ethics case assigned for class discussion. "What's the point of making us guess what the exam questions will be?" asked one of the undergrads at the start of class. "That's just the way it works in academe," Greg replied.

The next day's case focused on whistle-blowing. From the case and supplemental readings, the students did an excellent job of teasing out criteria for instances in which whistle-blowing was justified and when it was not. Greg told them he was pleased with their work.

"Most people tend to think of themselves as morally responsible if they are just doing their assigned tasks," Greg concluded. "But as you can see from this case, if people see their roles more broadly—as being agents of the company regardless of specific job descriptions—then it follows that they have a responsibility to respond when they notice that someone is acting in ways that could harm the company."

"You sound like such a hypocrite when you talk about what people in corporations should do!" Steven exploded. "Don't you know about other faculty here who are not meeting their responsibilities? Just what have you done to respond to that?"

Greg was as struck by the exasperation in Steven's voice as he was by the content of the questions. Just what was this guy's problem?

"Steven, this is a class in business ethics," Greg said calmly, "let's stick to the subject." But as the students filed silently from the classroom, Greg had the impression that the students sided with Steven rather than with him. And he just felt odd. Steven and the others were not really questioning his authority. It felt more as though they were questioning his ethics.

Although neither Greg Johnson nor his students has yet labeled the elephant standing in the classroom, its presence is undeniable. The message is that we can't exempt the classroom itself from ethical exploration.

In professional ethics literature, questions related to the ethics of ethics education have largely focused on concerns about whether teachers who advocate particular positions are in danger of indoctrinating their students and what, if anything, the teacher ought to model. This chapter explores those issues but also takes a look at the classroom and higher-education environment in which ethics is being taught. The ethics classroom is itself a living case for analysis, as is the institution of higher education in which it lives. The professor-student relationship is analogous to many other professional-client relationships. Teachers and students brave enough to address the ethical issues of higher education as they arise in situ are truly doing ethics in the first person.

VALUES AND ETHICS EDUCATION

The concern that an ethics teacher might indoctrinate students to his or her point of view has long been raised as an ethical issue of teaching ethics. Philosopher Ruth Macklin wrote in 1980, "A teacher of ethics may well have a commitment to one or more ideologies or normative theories, and yet hold that tolerance for the values of others requires that we let a hundred flowers bloom on the plains of value."[1]

Macklin distinguishes between teaching ethics and moral education. "[I]t is necessary to make a distinction between the teaching of ethics, on the one hand, and moral instruction, on the other. Moral instruction is an activity whose overriding aim is to get students to accept and act on a specific set of moral beliefs or principles. Unlike formal ethics teaching, it usually does not involve a critical examination of alternative principles, or any attempt to develop moral reasoning."[2]

Macklin states the accepted belief of the 1970s and 1980s that practical ethics teaching was not in itself value-laden. Yet it certainly was and is. Imagine the difference between someone who supports her conclusion with a well-reasoned argument as compared with someone who says, "This is right because I think it is right." The educational enterprise values well-justified conclusions over simple statements of opinion.

Teachers and students must follow certain conventional rules if ethics is to be taught and learned, including the following:

1. Reasons are necessary for the justified holding of a normative judgment.
2. One must be able to articulate one's reasons for holding a normative judgment.
3. The production of normative judgment and reason must be the result of the person's own deliberation.

4. One must respect and tolerate the views and reasoned judgments of others, even if one disagrees.

The search for reasons and justification is the principal distinction between teaching ethics and indoctrinating students to a particular point of view. But whether teachers of ethics should express their own carefully reasoned points of view is a matter of debate among scholars.

Some teachers favor a position of neutrality, some argue for reasoned advocacy, and others search for a middle ground.

ADVOCACY AND NEUTRALITY

Classical neutrality "recommends an instructional posture of nondisclosure on controversial issues, and procedural policies of balance and impartiality in handling competing viewpoints. According to classical neutrality, a teacher should not disclose her own position during class discussions of controversial issues."[3]

Those who argue against classical neutrality believe that attempts to hide one's views may distract students from developing their own reasoned points of view. According to ethics scholar Karen Hanson,

> Even when there is a careful attempt to proceed as if from a point of neutrality, when required readings are scrupulously "balanced" and when equal time is devoted to the exposition of the best arguments for and against all leading contentions in the debate, the professor may find that students become curious about which side is in fact embraced by an "authority" who can, apparently, survey clearly the entire field. Indeed, by keeping his or her opinions cloaked, the teacher may sometimes make those opinions more intriguing, so that students become perversely focused not on grasping a range of argumentation but on solving the particular, and personal, enigma of the professor's private opinion.[4]

Some argue that the teacher ought to advocate for his own reasoned judgment because this advocacy models what the students should be doing. Michel Golden states that the teacher who openly advocates a substantive moral position in an age of unreflective moral skepticism serves as "not merely a model of honesty, but a model of self-assurance, pride, and individuality."[5]

According to scholars Gloria Albrecht and Leonard Weber,

> [F]aculty in the classroom need to model what they want students to learn in the class. Students should observe faculty demonstrating what it means to be ethically sensitive and ethically educated citizens and members of particular professions. One

cannot model ethical sensitivity without identifying what one personally sees as the ethical dimensions of particular situations. One cannot model decision-making skills involving ethical issues without taking positions on what should be done in particular circumstances. One cannot be a model in ethics and seek to be neutral.[6]

Linda Bomstad and Stephen Esquith both offer a middle ground between neutrality and advocacy for the ethics teacher. Bomstad says:

> Procedural neutrality demands that opposing points of view receive fair hearing: when we try to achieve this we send the message to students that important and relevant points of view deserve equal consideration. . . . Instead of modeling tentatively held value commitments, procedural neutrality is just as likely to model a deeply held commitment to rational inquiry, to withhold judgment on controversial issues until we have been enlightened by the best evidence.[7]

Like Bomstad, Esquith searches for an alternative to choosing between neutrality and position advocacy.

> For many students, taking sides is premature. For many questions, the very notion of opposing sides is problematic. It may be much more important to teach students how sides are defined and changed than how to defend one side or another at this point in their intellectual development.[8]

Esquith suggests that ethics instructors teach students how to formulate good questions rather than reach for conclusions.

> A discussion of questions can slow students down so that they can criticize or defend their own reactions to the material more than they usually do when they are simply absorbing a lecture or caught up in the heat of a debate.[9]

However, Bomstad and Esquith have not resolved the ethical issue any better than those who advocate neutrality or advocacy. The instructor who stands apart from the issues under consideration teaches her students to do the same. The instructor who teaches the students to formulate questions without giving them the opportunity to practice developing answers also models a lack of commitment to taking a position. The instructor who offers her well-reasoned conclusions may be perceived as implying that students should claim that position as well.

THE NEED FOR INSTRUCTOR TRANSPARENCY

In the case study that opens this chapter, Greg Johnson takes the position of the advocate. Whether the ethics teacher chooses a neutral stance, one of advocacy, or one that avoids anyone's arguing for a particular position, it is important for instructors to be clear with themselves and with their students about what choice they are making and why.

The students confronting Greg were asking for him to explain and defend the choices he had made. They asked him to identify how the classroom was different in morally relevant ways from the corporation. Their confrontation actually demonstrated their belief that he was an ethical instructor as well as an instructor of ethics. Unfortunately, Greg was not prepared to explain his choices. Greg, like many college instructors, had accepted the conventions of higher education without question. Traditional students are likely to do the same. However, students who have been out of school for a while are less likely to do so. They have been successful in other work environments with different expectations and assumptions. But regardless of whether students have been out in the workforce, they are good at noticing when an instructor's actions do not conform to what the instructor says.

Expecting teachers of ethics to conform to the ethical responsibilities that they preach does not mean that teachers of ethics should be better behaved people than other faculty members. An ethical professional is one who is self-aware, self-reflective, and self-critical, not someone who always chooses the morally best action.

Modeling what it means to engage in case analysis in a reflective and rigorous way is only one of the many opportunities that ethics teachers have for modeling ethical commitment. How the ethics instructor designs a course and evaluation methods and how willing that instructor is to explain and justify choices set the ethical tone of the classroom.

No ethics teacher would accept "This is just the way that we do it" as being justification for another professional's decisions or for the basis of a student's analysis. Greg's students pointed out the inconsistency of Greg's suggesting that ethical corporations were those that had justifiable rules and procedures when he would not justify the rules in his own classroom.

In addition to the ethics classroom, the college or university is full of ethical land mines. Ethics in the first person may find instructors and their students wondering about any of the following:

The Classroom
  1. How clearly are goals articulated?
  2. How well do the activities of the class assist students in achieving those goals?
  3. How well do the methods of evaluation give students an opportunity to demonstrate that they have achieved the described learning goals?
  4. How do topics chosen and materials used reflect the instructor's val-

ues? How open is the instructor in explaining to the class why some topics or materials are included and others are not?

5. Has the instructor articulated the students' rights and responsibilities?

The Professional Professor

1. What are the professor's rights and responsibilities? How are those articulated to the students?
2. Does the professor define his or her responsibilities as being within the roles of teacher, researcher, and provider of service, or are those responsibilities seen more broadly as agents of the institution? How does the difference change perception of professional responsibilities?

The Ethics of the Environment

1. How well does the college or university stand up to ethical scrutiny?
2. Are students given the opportunity to examine issues in their own backyards? Whatever the professional or practical area under consideration, there are possibilities for case development and analysis within the institution of higher education and in the community just outside its gates.
3. Are administrators and faculty open to having their choices examined? It is difficult to help students believe that ethical analysis makes a difference in the real world if the community of higher education is exempt.

The ethics instructor instructing ethically is one who exemplifies the characteristics that the teacher hopes to promote. Just as it is reasonable to expect that a professor who teaches editing produce course documents free of typographical and grammatical errors, it is reasonable to expect that the teacher of ethics will be someone who takes the ethics of his or her own practice seriously.

NOTES

1. Ruth Macklin, "Problems in the Teaching of Ethics," in *Ethics Teaching in Higher Education*, ed. Daniel Callahan and Sissela Bok (New York: Plenum, 1980), 82.
2. Macklin, "Problems," 90.
3. Linda Bomstad, "Advocating Procedural Neutrality," *Teaching Philosophy* 18, no. 3 (1995): 197.

4. Karen Hanson, "Between Apathy and Advocacy: Teaching and Modeling Ethical Reflection," *Ethical Dimensions of College and University Teaching*, no. 66 (1996): 4.

5. Michel Golden, *Teaching Philosophy* 4, no. 1 (1981): 9, quoted in Stephen Esquith, "How Neutral Is Discussion," *Teaching Philosophy* 11, no. 3 (1988): 193–208.

6. Gloria Albrecht and Leonard J. Weber, "Personal Commitments, Privileged Positions and the Teaching of Applied Ethics," *Professional Ethics* 3, nos. 3 & 4 (1994): 141–155; 143.

7. Bomstad, "Advocating," 203.

8. Stephen Esquith, "How Neutral Is Discussion," *Teaching Philosophy* 11, no. 3 (1988): 193–208.

9. Esquith, "How Neutral," 203.

Chapter Three

Aspirations, Activities, and Assessment

From the 1970s, when I taught high school, I've always welcomed different student points of view. At least that's what I *thought* I knew about myself until I encountered a student in my early years of college teaching who challenged my tolerance. Her resistance made my own bias painfully obvious.

I remember wondering the first day of the semester if Dinka Poe would be trouble.[1] That day, I watched with interest as the students drifted into the classroom for a junior-level course in professional ethics. According to the presemester roster, which was good for a rough guess of who might actually be in the class, I expected to see thirty students, equally split between the genders. Most of those registered were sophomores and juniors, along with a handful of seniors and a handful of freshmen.

I smiled as I noticed people with different skin shades, ethnic features, dress styles, and ages. I had found that a variety of life experiences among the students meant that different views would emerge naturally in discussions.

Then Dinka Poe walked into the room.

Dinka wore the dress of a traditional religious group. I didn't know much about the particular religion, but I wondered what it would do to class discussion if Dinka was dogmatic or if she held beliefs that were very different from those of the other students.

I handed out the syllabus and explained my primary learning objectives for the class. "I want you to be engaged, with your heart and with your gut, with things that you care about. I want you to be provoked into a critical and intellectual examination of your beliefs and the beliefs of others. And, as ethics happens best in conversation, it is important to me that you learn to talk with others in the process of doing ethical thinking."

I explained that students would work in collaborative groups to examine controversies in professions of their choice and would also examine issues that they personally found morally compelling. As the students were still very attentive, I purposely asked a big question: "So, what kinds of things do you care about? Is there some issue that really bugs you?"

I wanted to see how brave the students were. I wanted to see if they were ready to engage.

The students rewarded me by giving me what I call "popcorn responses." Silence, and then first one, then another, then three, and suddenly they were talking over one another in their hurry to be heard.

After ten minutes, and comments from about half the group, I asked my next question, "So, what makes these *ethical* issues?" I was able to coax comments about job responsibilities and concerns about how individuals should be treated. I was happy. We were on our way to becoming a learning community.

I told them they were great and then waited to see if someone else would speak. I found that if I gave the more quiet students another chance, some of them found the courage to add their perspectives.

Dinka Poe spoke. "And what do you do, Professor," Dinka asked, "if there are students who do not wish to challenge or change their beliefs?"

That was an easy question, made easier by my recent rereading of John Stuart Mill's essay *On Liberty*. "Changing your beliefs is not necessary," I said, "but challenging them is. As the British philosopher, John Stuart Mill taught us, you don't really know for sure what you believe until you see how well those beliefs stand against opposing or contradictory opinion."

Dinka responded thoughtfully, "I have had plenty of opportunities to see how my beliefs hold up against the opinions of others. I am comfortable with the beliefs I hold and do not want them challenged. What can you tell us about the cultural and religious ideologies that philosopher Mill was expressing in his writings?"

Off the top of my head, I realized that I didn't have an answer, but I decided that the question was irrelevant. "What's important," I said, "is not his religion or his culture but how well his philosophical arguments withstand the test of time."

"And that, Professor, is where you and I disagree."

Dinka told us more about herself over the next month. At first, the students and I felt privileged to hear how an intentional community functioned within our heterogeneous culture. Dinka was completing a degree in education because she wanted to do a good job of teaching her children, at least through early childhood. The children might or might not be homeschooled after that.

Dinka's major required this course, and she took it reluctantly. As long as Dinka could keep a personal distance from the subject matter, she was willing to dissect and analyze arguments. But when asked to make a normative judgment, Dinka said or wrote, "Trust in God."

It is an understatement to say that Dinka's presence made a difference in the class. After that first month of fascination with Dinka's way of life, I realized that each class meeting felt increasingly disconnected and difficult. Dinka refused to engage at the level I thought necessary, and the other students were affected by her reluctance. It occurred to me that Dinka thought she was doing God's work through her polite but unflinching disruption of my teaching plans.

I was interested in her impact but was also concerned about the disintegration of our process. Fewer students were willing to argue a position or even to state a point of view.

Then, the students became angry with me. Some of them seemed to think that my probing questions set them up for Dinka's religious pronouncements. But others were beginning to take the stand that it was wrong to judge others. "As long as you're not getting in my way, you should be able to do whatever you want," was how one student summed it up. "What right do you have," asked another, "to say that your way is the right way?"

That was when I started counting down the number of class periods until the end of the semester.

Dinka and her classmates forced me to question my own beliefs about what I was teaching and to think again about how I justified to students the choices I made in teaching ethics.

Dinka was able to call into question my learning objectives, method of pedagogy, and assessment techniques. At the time, I didn't think about the situation in that way. But this chapter grew from my being forced to think about how ethics should be taught. Just as my ideas about that have matured, the perspectives of the teaching ethics profession have matured as well.

In this chapter, I describe a three-part curriculum for ethics education: aspirations, activities, and assessment (AAA). The AAA approach is based on the belief that these three steps are essential and interdependent. Aspirations describe the teaching and learning goals and objectives. Activities describe how students are expected to reach those aspirations. Assessment is the process by which students can demonstrate, most particularly to themselves, that they have achieved the learning goals and objectives.

ASPIRATIONS: THE HASTINGS CENTER'S GOALS

In the late 1970s, the Hastings Center task forces articulated a set of goals for teaching practical ethics. Those goals are like midlevel ethical principles. They neither state foundational rules nor supply clear direction for what teachers or students ought to specifically do in the classroom. However, the goals provide a set of standards that instructors can use as guidelines for developing their own course direction and that students can use to measure their own progress in the class.

The Hastings Center's goals were written in response to skeptics at the time. Skeptics wondered *whose* ethics would be taught and how teachers could evaluate the results of ethics instruction without imposing their own personal moral judgments.

In addition, there was tension between those who argued that ethics was a purely intellectual exercise and those who wanted ethics teaching to result in "good" professionals or generally "better" people.

According to Daniel Callahan,

> It is often said that one test of the success of teaching ethics would be a change in the moral behavior of students, and that a central goal should thus be an attempt to change behavior. If ethics bears on conduct, then the point of teaching ethics should be to influence conduct. That seems clear and simple enough. Upon closer inspection, however, this is an exceedingly dubious goal. First, even if a course could change behavior, it is hard to see how, short of constant reinforcement of the new behavior, its effect could be long or surely sustained once outside of the classroom; other influences would play their role, and no course can be a permanent antidote against them. Second, in most types of course [sic] in applied or professional ethics, the students will not yet have had an opportunity to behave one way or another; there is nothing to change, since their moral behavior, for better or worse, still lies before them.[2]

Callahan eschewed the notion of "moral education" in the teaching of practical ethics if what was meant by that was "the goal of improving moral behavior, instilling certain virtues and traits of character, and developing morally responsible persons."[3]

Callahan cautioned that if students were found, at the end of the course, to agree with their instructor's perspective, one should not conclude that indoctrination had taken place. "The real question is whether the students have come to those convictions by means of the use of analytical tools and skills that might have led them in other directions."[4]

According to Callahan, "That no teacher can have a full grasp of the truth does not imply that there is no final moral truth."[5]

The Hastings Center's goals were intended to ensure that courses would be neither simply intellectual exercises nor an inculcation of particular values. In the words of the center, they are intended to be goals "that are important for all courses in ethics, whatever the educational level or context":

1. Stimulating the moral imagination. "Students must be provoked to understand that there is a moral point of view, that human beings live their lives in a web of moral relationships, that a consequence of moral theories and rules can be either suffering or happiness (or, usually, some combination of both), that the moral dimensions of life are often hidden as visible, and that moral choices are inevitable and often difficult."[6]

2. Recognizing ethics issues. "[T]he goal of a recognition of ethical issues [is] a conscious, rational attempt to sort out those elements in emotional responses that represent appraisal and judgment, however inchoate at first."[7]

3. Eliciting a sense of moral obligation. "One could merely analyze the logical implications of moral propositions. But apart from that kind of exercise, a major point of ethics is that of the guidance of conduct, not only how I ought to direct my behavior toward others, but also what I ought to be able to claim from others in their behavior toward me."[8]

4. Developing analytical skills. "If concepts, rules and principles are the tools of rationality in ethics, then skills must be developed in using them. . . . Coherence and consistency are minimal goals, both in the analysis of ethical propositions and in their justification."[9]

5. Tolerating—and reducing—disagreement and ambiguity. "Some disagreement in ethics is inevitable, but some is not; only great care and attention will make it possible to sort out the difference, whether it is a matter of ethical theory or the resolution of concrete moral dilemmas. Learning to argue without rancor, and to disagree without personal invective, are important skills to be developed."[10]

The goals make clear that students ought to approach their work in practical ethics as something more than an intellectual puzzle. Yet the goals provide some comfort for those worried that charismatic ethics teachers with evil intent would produce clones. The first three goals assume the existence of the moral point of view. The final two goals imply that there are identifiable better and worse ways of working within the moral sphere.

Twenty-five years later, the Hastings Center's goals can be further refined to reflect how practical ethics has matured. Thoughtful instructors still grapple with creating reasonable expectations for the ultimate outcomes of practical ethics courses. Even if the field had been initially developed on the belief that such courses could create a better world or more ethical professionals, it is safe to say that the experiment has failed. Regardless of all the ethics courses taught, there are still those individuals who knowingly choose to do the wrong thing.

Instructional Objectives Versus Pedagogical Hope

Practical ethics courses cannot make bad people good, nor can these courses create ethical professionals. As Callahan pointed out, many of the professional ethics courses are taught to preprofessionals, students who still have their professional choices and their professional mistakes ahead of them.

It is truly a leap of faith to believe that the greater sophistication that students develop in the ethics class will turn into more ethical professional or personal decision making in the future. Many practical ethics instructors have heard from former students who, years after the fact, have suddenly seen the relevance of the class to their current work. On the other hand, many of us have given As to students who have later demonstrated the worst of ethical choices at some time in their professional careers. The one thing we can be sure of is that classes in practical ethics help students develop greater sophistication in how they approach ethical questions in the here and now.

Regardless of what the future holds for those who take courses in practical ethics, there is a connection between having the ability to deal with ethical questions in a cognitively complex way and being aware of most or all of the morally relevant factors. One can certainly stumble into doing the right thing, or an accidental action may turn out in a way that doesn't cause harm. However, if one *can* reason carefully about the ethical dimensions of a problem, it is more likely that that person *will* reason carefully.

Instructional objectives describe the level of sophistication the instructor expects students to achieve. These objectives also imply how students can show that they have achieved the teacher's goals (aspirations). Objectives set out what the students can hope to accomplish by taking the class.

Instructional objectives are different from pedagogical hope. An instructor's pedagogical hope expresses possibilities for what students might do with their learning in the future. An ethics instructor might hope that her students some day choose the tough-but-best thing to do, against tremendous odds and even at tremendous cost to themselves. Another instructor might hope that a student use his new insights to make the profession he enters a more ethical institution.

The pedagogical hope for the music instructor that her students perform majestically or the pedagogical hope for the English teacher that his students write inspired prose and poetry serve as inspiration for teachers and students alike. In the same way, the pedagogical hope that ethics students will become people who make the world a little better inspires ethics instruction. But inspiration is neither the basis for course planning nor for assessment.

Student Competencies in Practical Ethics Courses

The Hastings Center's goals can be rewritten to fit with the outcomes-based focus of most universities and accreditation councils of the twenty-first century. Outcomes-based instruction calls for demonstrable student behaviors.

If instructors "stimulate the moral imagination," students can reasonably be expected to express approval or disapproval, pleasure or outrage appropriately in response to real-life situations they encounter. Moral imagination involves more than the intellect. Analysis can be cool and dispassionate, but imagination involves integration of the gut and heart with the rational abilities. Students should leave the practical ethics course caring about what happens in particular situations and feeling called to action or, at least, called to analysis by the presentation of those cases.

If "recognizing ethical issues" is something that should occur, then students should leave the course with the ability to distinguish decisions made on an ethical basis from other kinds of decision making. Failure to distinguish ethical aspects from legal, religious, economic, or prudential aspects of a quandary is a common problem in real-life reasoning. For example, when a reader (or an editor) laments the decision of a news manager to publish an ethically questionable story or photo by saying, "Oh, all the owners care about is the bottom line!" the complainant has erroneously responded to an ethical issue—the societal responsibilities of news organizations—by referring to an economic reality.[11]

At the end of a course in practical ethics, students should be able to notice deviation from discussions of ethically relevant factors and should be able to keep their own reasoning in the ethical sphere.

"Eliciting a sense of moral obligation" is the struggle to do ethics in the first person. It is relatively easy for all of us to analyze what some other person did wrong or what that person should do differently if given the opportunity to try again. It is far more challenging to stay centered in our own moral agency and strive to be clear on what we have the power and responsibility to affect. It is more difficult to address issues as if we were the persons affected.

If instructors are interested in students' "developing analytic skills," then they will look for competency in what is also called critical thinking. Successful students will be able to dissect an argument in everyday language and parse out the conclusion, the premises, and the assumptions. They will be able to analyze the soundness or the cogency of the argument through an examination of the argument's structure and content, as well as factors ignored by the argument.

The final Hastings Center goal, "tolerating—and reducing—disagreement and ambiguity," is a delicious statement in that it illustrates what it describes. What it means to simultaneously tolerate and reduce ambiguity is, well, ambiguous. Students should be able to recognize and express the tension between *tolerating* and *reducing* disagreement and ambiguity. Students who have reached a level of competency with this goal can identify where those engaged in an ethics discussion agree and where they do not. They can identify what would be necessary to bring about more agreement among the discussants, as well as identify where there is not likely to be agreement.

For example, the crux of the abortion debate is the question of when a fetus deserves the same moral protections as a born person. At conception? Even if that conception occurs in a petri dish? At the moment of birth? But not the moment before? Agreement on that question would make it relatively easy to determine when it is morally permitted to cause the death of a human embryo or fetus. But we do not have agreement on the answers to these questions.

Nevertheless, public policy must be made, regardless of the ongoing ambiguity of exactly when a fetus should count as a person. Disagreement and ambiguity must be both tolerated and reduced.

Additional Goals for Teaching Ethics

The following teaching goals for practical ethics courses are meant to further flesh out what was offered by the Hastings Center. Courses in practical ethics should do the following:

1. Help students become aware of the values they use in determining how they do behave, and how they should behave, toward people and toward other subjects of moral worth. Help them identify relevant role-related responsibilities and help them compare and contrast their own personal values with those of the profession or other role expectations.
2. Raise students' consciousness concerning occasions for ethical discussions. Create opportunities for them to differentiate the moral sphere from other decision-making spheres such as law, economics, personal opinion, and religion.
3. Give students practice in analyzing tough philosophical concepts such as confidentiality, privacy, justice, deception, promise keeping, moral causality, blameworthiness, and praiseworthiness. Teach them the difference between moral permissibility and moral requirement and the difference between minimal and ideal ethical choices.
4. Introduce students to the finest relevant writings on ethical theories,

problems, and processes for analysis that are available from the philosophical traditions, the area of ethical concern, and other sources.

5. Teach them a process for systematic moral analysis that includes techniques for developing creative alternatives for dealing with ethical concerns.

6. Above all, plan activities that require students and teachers to be self-aware, self-reflective, and self-critical.

ACTIVITIES: METHODS FOR ACHIEVING ASPIRATIONS

The methods for teaching courses in practical ethics should reflect the talents and sensibilities of instructors as well as needs dictated by content and students. The most effective instructors can vary their teaching methods to match the learning methods that are most effective for their individual students. But there is no one right way to teach ethics.

Good ethics teaching can happen through lecture as long as there is also an opportunity for students to try out their own thinking and to hear the views of others. Effective ethics teaching can happen through case discussion as long as there is an opportunity for students to assimilate content material and structures for moral reasoning as well as talk about dilemmas.

Both methods can be misused or ineffective. However, activities must fit with the teacher's aspirations. For example, it makes little sense for instructors to claim that their learning goal is for students to analyze the structure and content of arguments unless students are offered the opportunity to practice those specific skills.

ASSESSMENT

Objectives (which are developed from aspirations) imply both activities by which the objectives can be achieved and methods for how achievement can be assessed. Consider the following objective:

Students will develop a counterargument to a stated thesis and propose a synthesis that includes valid points from both thesis and antithesis.

The instructor could have students demonstrate this learning by writing an essay in response to a well-written ethical argument with which they disagree. They could distinguish valid points from those they find less valid. They could identify alternative responses that recognize valid points in the presenting argument and in their response.

Those who worry about whether the teacher can be fair in evaluating students who hold conclusions contrary to their own should begin by examining learning objectives. Here is where the nuggets of transparent assessment can be found.

One of the best sources for evaluation are students themselves. Learning ethics presupposes a new level of self-awareness. That makes self-assessment a particularly appropriate tool for this field.

It is important for students to demonstrate to the instructor what they have learned about ethical decision making, but a product for the teacher will not make them more sophisticated decision makers. The best assessment techniques will show that students are aware of how their ability to think ethically has changed.

One straightforward way for students to demonstrate their awareness of what they have learned is through the use of pre- and posttest measures. In my classes, students are asked, as a pretest at the start of the term, to provide an analysis of the ethical dimensions of a particular case. At the end of the term, they are given their pretests back and asked to provide a meta-analysis of their initial essays. They are asked to describe how their understanding about the problem has changed from how they made sense of it at the start of the term. They are asked to describe how they might approach the problem differently now. They are asked to describe what has changed in how they think about the problem and why the change has occurred. In summary, they are asked to demonstrate to themselves and to me that they think differently about ethics now. The student's ability to respond thoughtfully to these questions illustrates the degree of self-recognized growth that each has achieved during the term.

Another approach for illustrating demonstrable change through ethics instruction is to ask students to create their own learning goals. These goals, developed at the start of the term, show that students understand the course objectives as well as provide them the opportunity to articulate their own relevant interests. Throughout the term, the learning goals can provide a basis for self-analysis. Questions students can consider include the following: Have your learning goals changed? Why? How well are you doing at achieving a particular goal? How can you show that development?

Self-assessment in practical ethics underscores the need for students to develop greater consciousness about themselves as decision makers and is consistent with the more general goals of higher education. If the expectation of higher education is that students finish their degree programs with the ability to be autonomous agents, they require practice to get there.

A CAUTION REGARDING SERVICE LEARNING

Some colleges have instituted *service learning* and have connected this with ethics education. Service learning, required in some settings and elective in others, links community service with course credit. The educators assume that ethical awareness can be developed through working for charities or non-profit organizations.

For example, the mission statement of the Service Learning Institute at California State University, Monterey Bay (CSUMB), reads, "The mission . . . is to foster and promote social justice by cultivating reciprocal service and learning partnerships among CSUMB students, faculty, staff and the surrounding tri-county community."[12] The school's academic program "is guided by the campus' Vision Statement that establishes 'coordinated community service' as a vehicle to enable students to develop the 'critical thinking abilities to be productive citizens, and the social responsibility and skills to be community builders.'"[13]

Florida International University says that service learning "fosters the development of those 'intangibles'—empathy, personal values, beliefs, awareness, self-esteem, self-confidence, social-responsibility, and helps to foster a sense of caring for others."[14]

Maybe. The connection between service learning and ethics is dubious, unless students are led through a critical examination of their service learning through the lens of personal and social ethics. Here is a collection of some of the faulty assumptions that underlie the belief that service learning is necessarily "ethical" education.

1. The United Way error. This is the faulty assumption that involvement with a community charity or nonprofit association necessarily engages students with an "ethical" organization. Not all social service agencies are doing their jobs. Even when a charitable or nonprofit organization is meeting responsibilities to its clients, the treatment of employees, the environment, or competitors may all be questionable. Students who do service learning should learn to critically analyze the ethics of the overall practice of organizations.

2. The questionable choice of philanthropy. Students who do service learning implicitly or explicitly support the fundamental principles of the agency where they volunteer. Yet the assumption that particular services should be provided through charities or nonprofits rather than government is an assumption that should be questioned. Some services that are delivered by charity in the United States are governmentally

supported elsewhere. Students should examine assumptions that lead one nation to have a service provided by government and another to have the same service provided by charity.

3. External acts promote internal development. Service-learning activities are designed primarily to promote the growth of the student. Here the faulty assumption is that external acts will promote internal development. For some students who find themselves in the right service-learning experience when they are ready for such growth, the assumption has validity. Other students may develop character or make personal moral progress more efficiently by taking further coursework in practical ethics or by participating in an "ethics bowl." There is no guarantee that a student engaged in service learning will think systematically or analytically about the experience. Some students will simply and nonreflectively put in the hours.

4. Faculty conflict of interest. Some schools encourage faculty to develop service-learning components in their classes by offering monetary compensation. If service learning is a fit for a particular course, the teacher should incorporate the activity without enticement. Imagine the faculty uproar if administration offered to pay $1,000 for including a particular textbook or corporate-sponsored teaching.

A RETURN TO DINKA POE

Returning to the teaching situation with Dinka Poe described at the beginning of this chapter, I would handle it differently now. Today, I would meet privately with Dinka to talk about the goals of my class and of higher education in general. Students at the postsecondary level should expect to have their worldviews challenged, shaken, and rearranged in the process of completing an undergraduate degree. They don't need to abandon religious beliefs or other deeply held convictions, but they do need to develop a deep understanding of the pluralism that is protected by the ideal of democracy. Students can't accomplish this goal without engaging with others and with others' beliefs.

Today, I could confidently tell Dinka that she could expect her grade to reflect her willingness to participate in the process. I would also feel safe to remind us both that neither of us needs to be defensive about our beliefs. Having our beliefs confronted by others who believe differently can lead to a reflexive defensiveness, as it did on my part at the time. At this point in my career, I tell students to expect to feel angry or defensive at some point in the class. And I tell them that feeling angry or defensive does not entitle them to be less than civil to someone who holds a different belief.

Now I would raise the matter openly in the classroom about what it is like to develop empathy with others who do not share our own personal and deeply held convictions. Students need to imagine what it might be like to believe something different from what they do believe if they are going to reach the Hastings Center goal of tolerating—and reducing—disagreement and ambiguity. Moral sophistication means, among other things, being able to engage in ethics discussions with those who have spiritual intuitions or transcendental leanings different from one's own. And for the secular students in the room, it means being able to try on a religious point of view.

Religion is not a necessary or sufficient condition for making good ethical decisions. It is a motivator for some and not for others. The reality of living in a pluralistic society means that one must be able to argue for how others should act based on something other than one's own religious beliefs. As the questions of how people should treat others extend across any number of religions or subcultures, the answers must be accessible on some basis other than spiritual beliefs or ethnic practices. Retreating to pat religious answers for difficult ethical problems can be as much an example of begging the question as substituting legal limitations (what one will be held legally accountable for doing) for ethical analysis (what one should do, regardless of legal accountability).

And while I am sure that my own mistaken beliefs and concerns continue to govern whatever relationships I have with students, I do not today think I would begin the semester fearful of Dinka Poe. I have learned that once I decide a student is going to be "trouble," the student invariably becomes what I expect to see.

NOTES

1. Identifying factors have been changed.
2. Daniel Callahan, "Goals in the Teaching of Ethics," in *Ethics Teaching in Higher Education*, ed. Daniel Callahan and Sissela Bok (New York: Plenum, 1980), 69.
3. Callahan, "Goals," 71.
4. Callahan, "Goals," 71–72.
5. Callahan, "Goals," 71.
6. Callahan, "Goals," 64–65.
7. Callahan, "Goals," 65.
8. Callahan, "Goals," 66.
9. Callahan, "Goals," 67.
10. Callahan, "Goals," 68.

11. The complainant has also moved the conversation from a normative question, "What *should* news organizations ethically do," to a descriptive answer, "This *is* what corporate owners care about."

12. California State University, Monterey Bay, "The Service Learning Institute (SLI)," service.csumb.edu (accessed October 3, 2005).

13. California State University, Monterey Bay, "Service Learning Institute Overview," service.csumb.edu/overview/overview.html (accessed October 3, 2005).

14. Florida International University, "Four Things Faculty Want to Know About!" www.fiu.edu/~time4chg/Library/fourthings.html (accessed October 3, 2005).

Chapter Four

The Theoretical Toolkit

The case that follows is based on a struggle that a participant presented at one of my workshops in teaching ethics. The outcome presented at the end of this chapter reflects suggestions that other participants made for how the instructor might have introduced classical philosophy differently in the practical ethics class. It is included to encourage teachers and students to make effective use of the tools that classical philosophy has to offer.

Thomas sighed as he surveyed the pile of media ethics case analyses that covered his desk. The assignment simply hadn't worked.

His learning goal was for students to incorporate the power of classical philosophy as they analyzed a case.

The case that Thomas wrote up for analysis was based on the personal experience of one of his former students. Thomas called the case "The Journalist Who Did Too Much." It described a very eager young journalist, just out of college, who put in extra hours in her brand new reporting job. The reporter, Sara Woo, found herself moved by the plight of her story subjects and often found ways to help them out. But she was now in trouble.

The union representative told Sara that she could not work more than her eight hours each day without claiming overtime. This policy surprised Sara and made her feel trapped between policy and her passion.

Sara did not want to ask for more money for her additional time. Sara knew that her inexperience made her slower than the other reporters. In addition, she was willing, at least for the present, to make journalism her life. Sara had moved cross-country to take this job. She really had no social life yet, and Sara thrived on the satisfaction she got from pursuing and writing stories. Sara loved seeing her byline in the paper, particularly when she got a front-page story. The managing editor had told her that her stories showed she was willing to go the extra mile.

Then the city editor told Sara that she was a great reporter, but from now on, when she was done reporting a story, it was over. It was not okay for her to check in on the pregnant drug addict she had interviewed; it was not acceptable for her to drop off a bag of groceries at the under-the-bridge cardboard shelter where her homeless-story subject lived. "You are a journalist," the editor said. "Your job is to tell the story. It is up to others in the community to take care of the problems. If the social workers or public agencies are not doing their jobs, then write about that!"

Both the union representative and the city editor told Sara that other reporters were complaining about her. "You are making those who have family responsibilities look bad," said the union rep. "Being a missionary rather than a reporter is not a good way to make friends in the newsroom," the editor concurred.

Sara was angry that her good efforts were being criticized rather than appreciated. The end of the case found Sara wondering if maybe she ought to look for a job at another paper where her efforts might be rewarded instead of criticized.

In Thomas's media ethics class, these seniors, on the verge of being in Sara's position themselves, seemed uncertain about how to approach the case. There was clearly a problem here, but they couldn't decide whose problem it might be or how to approach it. Sara was trying hard to be a good reporter. Was the union representative the problem? How about the city editor? Some students tentatively offered criticisms of these characters. A few pointed out that everyone seemed to have good intentions here. All the students looked to Thomas to see if they were on the right track.

Thomas carefully avoided giving them direction. He wanted the students to feel discomforted as they started on their assignment. The students had read the chapter in their media ethics textbook on classical moral theory. "I'm not going to help you out on this one," Thomas said. "You have a lot of philosophical advisers to help you think out this case. Your assignment is to apply philosophical reasoning to Sara's situation."

Thomas hadn't been entirely sure what to expect. His own grasp of classical philosophy was uncertain, at best. But as he read the shallow, glib use of philosophical theory in the student papers, even he could tell that the students had missed the mark.

One student concluded, "Sara should do what she wants with her time off and be true to herself. After all, Aristotle said that you should be all that you can be." Thomas winced when he read that. The textbook's four-paragraph summary on Aristotle had not included that phrase, but Thomas had used the slogan in an attempt to help the students understand Aristotle's notion of happiness as human self-actualization.

Another wrote, "Jesus said that you should feed the starving masses. Why shouldn't journalists do their share?" Thomas wasn't quite sure what Jesus was doing in the middle of a chapter on secular philosophers, but there he was. Was the reliance on a religious authority supposed to give an argument more weight than those that relied on the traditional classicists? Or less?

Other students chose other philosophers. "Kant says do your duty. Sara's duty is to report the news. If journalists tried to help everyone instead of just doing their duty, the paper would never come out." While Thomas was impressed that the student got the idea of universalizing maxims from the short description of categorical imperative included in the text, this analysis still seemed to miss the point.

"Mill said look at the consequences," wrote another. "If Sara doesn't do what her editor says, she'll be out of a job and not able to do the greatest good for the greatest number." "So, is providing for Sara's good in everyone's interest?" Thomas asked silently.

It seemed to Thomas that each of the students had shopped through the theories until they each found a sentence from a philosopher that provided a hanger for their own personal points of view. The philosopher advisers had provided these students no more than a grab bag of easy rationalizations. That wasn't the notion of classical philosophy that Thomas wanted to leave with the students, but he wasn't sure what he should expect. Why was he teaching the theories of these old dead guys anyway?

Classical moral philosophy is classically misused in the teaching of practical ethics. Textbooks throughout the fields of practical ethics (e.g., engineering, media, nursing, social work) most often include a cursory introductory chapter on classical theory that results in reducing the moral systems and theories to slogans.

The pro forma introductory chapter on classical theory is most usually an introduction to Aristotle, Kant, and Mill (virtue theory, deontology, and utilitarianism). The theories are often presented as three separate formulas that yield three different conclusions when examining a case. The three are usually presented with no historical or conceptual connection to explain why they are included. Sometimes, each theory is presented with its classical objection, leaving the nonphilosopher reader with the reasonable question of why such a flawed theory is presented in the first place.

Rarely does the text offer a description of the power that the theories bring to considerations of practical ethics or to the substantial agreement that has existed among philosophers throughout the ages.

Other texts avoid classical theory altogether. These authors rely on professional codes or statements of occupational standards as the foundations upon which the students' work in ethics is to rest. Professional pronouncements of how practitioners should behave are treated as first principles with no further justification needed or offered.

Neither of these approaches is adequate for practical ethics education. Introducing classical theory without an integrated approach leads to students' misusing or ignoring classical theory in their own analyses. On the other hand, teaching professional codes as though they provide first principles implicitly tells students that foundations for ethical reasoning are arbitrary and based on nothing more than contemporary conventions.

For both students and teachers of practical ethics, an introduction to classical moral philosophy can provide the following:

- Conceptual justification behind policy, codes, statements of standards, and conventional current modes of behavior
- The theoretical backing that supports the good reasons for the beliefs the people hold
- Alternative perspectives to those offered by professional or conventional behaviors
- Structured ethical analysis that parses an argument into premises and conclusion and shows how well premises lead to the purported conclusion

Taking courses in classical moral philosophy is one way to develop this background, but not the only way. Motivated learners can work through anthologies that cover the history of moral philosophy and can supplement that with a basic text in critical thinking.

This chapter does not substitute for a course in classical philosophy or for the equivalent of self-study. It is meant to identify some anchor concepts that can support systematic analysis in practical ethics.

Classical moral philosophy provides two fundamental tools for the teachers and students of practical ethics. The first is method, and the second is content.

PHILOSOPHICAL METHODOLOGY
AND PRACTICAL ETHICS

Western moral philosophy is rooted in rationality. While rationality is not the sole basis that one should use in working through ethical questions, it provides a standardized start.[1] Unlike religion, culture, and personal opinion, the ability to reason is species-inclusive. Human beings who have average intelligence and the cognitive development of most ten-year-olds are capable of using rationality in determining how others should treat them.

Listen to students in an elementary school class argue with their teacher about why it is unfair for her to punish the whole group for an individual child's indiscretion. Watch people in a crowded subway station react with indignation when a stranger jostles or pushes them aside when it would have been just as easy for the stranger to avoid contact. These are just a few of the innumerable times in which one person indicates to another, "You are causing me unjustified harm. It is wrong for you to cause me harm unless you've got good reason for doing so."

Consider the nationwide rage and worldwide sympathy in response to the terrorist attacks of September 11, 2001. The reason that terrorism has power is that such acts are counterintuitive to the belief that one should not be harmed without reason. Acts of terrorism make people fear being harmed when there is seemingly no good reason for them to be harmed. Citizens who perceive themselves as having no direct control over their government reasonably expect that they will not be killed by those who denounce that government.

Terrorism is wrong because it subjects innocent victims to unjustified harm and causes other innocent citizens to fear being caused unjustified harm. Terrorism defies our reasonable belief that others should not cause us unjustified harm.

Rationality serves as the communication and behavioral bridge between human beings. The connection between wanting to protect oneself and understanding that one is capable of causing harm to others is what I call the *human analogy*. I recognize that other people are like me in that they wish not to be harmed without good reason. I recognize that other people are like me in that they can suffer death and other harms.

Because I, and all other competent adults, understand the human analogy, both torture and the Universal Declaration of Human Rights make sense. We can understand what it means for others to be harmed without reason. We can understand what it means to declare that others should not be caused harm. The human analogy implies that it is morally prohibited to cause others what is irrational to want for oneself or for others for whom one cares.[2]

Rationality goes beyond recognizing what one wishes to avoid, however. Rationality is also used in a less technical way to refer to how we make sense of the world. Human beings of average intelligence and cognitive development come hardwired with basic rules of logic.[3] Logical process is the basic form of philosophical method.

Even a child as young as two or three can reason through the logical implication when her mom says, "If you hit your sister, you'll get spanked." In fact, the child in question conducts a rather fancy reasoning process called modus tollens. The formal description of the child's reasoning goes something like this: "I want to hit my sister. I don't want to be spanked. I don't want to be spanked more than I want to hit my sister. Therefore, as I wish *not* to be spanked, I will not hit my sister."

This amazing little logician has constructed what philosophers call an *argument*. The word argument is used in a technical way to mean a set of one or more *premises* accompanied by a *conclusion*. The *premises* provide the collection of reasons that one has for believing or acting on a *conclusion*.

Arguments can be separated into premises, and they can be analyzed in two ways: structurally and in terms of content. A *structural* analysis may show whether the argument is *valid*; a *content* analysis will show whether the individual premises and conclusion are *true*; structural and content analyses together will show whether the argument is *sound*. *Cogency* is also important to consider in ethical arguments. Cogency asks us to consider whether the argument takes all evidence, both in support and not in support of the conclusion, into account. Cogency is important to consider even if the argument is sound.

An argument can be structurally valid and not provide a particularly good reason for holding the conclusion. Consider the following:

P1: Women have the legal right to control the use of their bodies.
P2: A developing fetus is part of a woman's body.
Therefore, women have the legal right to do what they want with a developing fetus.

This argument is structurally valid. P1 and P2 are both true premises, and the conclusion necessarily follows from those statements. However, moving on to a content analysis, the argument lacks cogency in that the premises leave out relevant information. Women do not have an absolute legal right to control the use of their bodies. They are not legally permitted (in most states) to choose to be sex workers. They are not legally permitted, anywhere in the United States, to sell a kidney or other body part to the highest bidder. And while the developing fetus is, indeed, part of the woman for the period of gestation, the developing fetus is different in kind from the woman's heart or hair or leg. Unlike these other parts, most fetuses are expected to reach a state in which they can live without dependency on their woman-hosts. The closer the fetus gets to that ability to survive independently, the more right it has to be considered as a separate entity rather than simply as a body part of the pregnant woman. So this argument is valid, but it is neither strong nor cogent.[4]

The most common error of reasoning comes from those who believe that their opinion makes their conclusion right. For example, consider the conclusion "Abortion is a woman's moral right." Well, maybe. That conclusion is the basis from which one can build back an argument. But when the holder of that conclusion explains that her reasoning is "It's just what I think," there is just cause for taking issue with the argument. Even if the person does, indeed, believe that abortion is a woman's right, it does not provide a good reason for arguing that the conclusion is objectively true.

Better arguments might include premises that no one should be able to force a woman to gestate a fetus against her will as this would be a type of assault. Counterarguments might seek to show how abortion is disanalogous with other examples of bodily privacy. Arguments by analogy (and disanalogy) are particularly appropriate in the work of practical ethics because, when confronted with a new or different problem, we have reasoning about similar questions with which to appeal.

As part of our rationality, human beings naturally strive for *consistency* and *generalizability*—or what philosophers call *universalizability*. *Consistency* means that we strive to make the same kind of normative judgments in cases that are similar in morally relevant ways. *Generalizability* means that we are willing to prescribe that others should choose in ways similar to ours.

Except when we're not. There are times when people ignore consistency and generalizability. Almost all of us have held on stubbornly to a point of view in a disagreement, even after it is pointed out to us that this view is inconsistent with others that we hold. We all have wished that some general rule be lifted in regard to our own special need or desire; we all might like to be exceptions to the case when the outcome is in our favor. But, in our better moments, the morally sophisticated among us realize that these choices were not the best.

The general process of everyday moral decision making is one of consistency and generalizability, despite our human flaws in attaining these goals. For example, it is important to me that I am treated no worse than other professors at my institution. Even if I think we are all underpaid and overworked, I am not, individually, being treated unethically if I am being treated in a consistent manner that is no different from the rest. But if I begin to see that others are getting special privileges without a morally relevant difference in our situations, I have reason for thinking I am a victim of unethical treatment. I also generalize that no other professors should get better treatment than their peers without having a morally relevant distinction to back up their case.

Methodologically speaking, grounding in philosophical analysis gives the teacher and student of practical ethics tools to assist in formulating and critiquing arguments.

A PRIMER ON CLASSICAL MORAL THEORY

An ethical theory attempts to provide a general test for how people should act and a process to use for evaluating our actions and the actions of others. An adequate theory will provide definitions for morally rich terms such as *good, bad, right, wrong, harms,* and *justification.* It will provide reasons for why people should choose to act morally when they can choose to do otherwise. An adequate theory will address a range of human actions and offer guiding principles or rules that link the theoretical understandings with how real people could actually live their lives.

Ethical theories are normative as well as descriptive. The theories are descriptive in that they seek to explain how and why people behave as they do. Theories are normative in that they also seek to describe how people should behave, rather than simply how they do behave.

As ethical theories express prescriptions for human behavior, it is necessary that they describe possible human behaviors. For example, if a theory states that "individuals should take into account the rights and needs of others," it follows, by pragmatic implication, that sometimes individuals can act in this way and are likely to be found praiseworthy when they do. The prescription of how one ought to act will reflect something more like a prototype of human behavior—that is, what is possible and ethically permitted or ideal.

In this way, ethical theories are like grammatical theories. Contemporary philosopher Bernard Gert explains the similarity this way:

> A useful analogy for knowledge of morality is knowledge of the grammar that all competent speakers of a language have. Even though almost no competent speaker can explicitly describe the grammatical system, all competent speakers know it in the sense that they use it when speaking and when interpreting the speech of others. . . . An explicit account of a grammar must accurately describe the way competent speakers actually use the language.[5]

Grammar theories and systems are descriptive in that they provide a prototype of competent speakers speaking well. One of the descriptive rules by which English is usually spoken is this: *The subject of the sentence comes before the verb.* But the same descriptive statement becomes *prescriptive* when it helps a new speaker learn how to use the language. Even competent speakers may need to reason out the rules from time to time. "Now, is *when* or *if* the best usage in the previous sentence?" I ask myself.

Like grammar, an ethical theory will describe what it looks like for competent individuals to be acting well in regard to others. The theory will not describe how all people act all of the time. People make mistakes in their choices of action or purposefully do wrong, just as they sometimes make grammatical errors or purposefully use substandard English.

For analysis to take place, all ethical theories require a *fundamental moral unit*. The fundamental moral unit is the object worthy of primary moral protection. The three classical Western theories most usually taught in the practical ethics classroom (Aristotle's virtue theory, Kant's deontology, and Mill's utilitarianism) begin with the assumption that the individual person is the fundamental moral unit. Ethics, within this conception, is a set of rules that prescribes how strangers should treat other strangers. I have my rights and you have your rights. Western ethical theories tell us how to be our best individual selves without intruding on one another's rights.

All three major theories include an understanding that it is prima facie wrong to cause other people harm. All three include a prohibition against causing harm for no good reason. In addition, the theories go beyond this moral minimalism and argue that people should also act in ways that promote good.

The three theories include a universality requirement. Universality requires that the theory prescribes or proscribes action for all people who might find themselves in a similar situation. Although all three have a universality requirement, only one is *absolutist*. An absolutist theory is one that dictates that an action is always wrong, with no exceptions. For example, Immanuel Kant's moral prohibition against lying is absolute. Kant says that it is just simply wrong to lie, ever. Kant knows that everyone (even the great philosopher himself!) will make moral mistakes in this regard, and he also provides a fair amount of wiggle room in helping people ethically choose not to say the truth.[6] But in the end, when someone speaks or acts with the intent of leading another to a false conclusion, it is a lie. Kant argues that it is important for all people to realize and accept that they have done something wrong in those instances in which they choose to lie. Even if the lie helped prevent a larger harm, according to Kant, it would have been better to choose action that didn't include lying.

A theory can be *universal* without being absolutist if it has a standard range of exceptions. A universal theory can state that people should generally act in some particular way but shows under which conditions exceptions should be allowed.

APPLYING MORAL THEORY TO THE TEACHING
AND LEARNING OF PRACTICAL ETHICS

There are good reasons for Aristotle, Kant, and Mill to be the theorists most often taught for application to practical ethics in that they bring three major aspects of ethical analysis: evaluation of the agent and the search for middle ground (from Aristotle), the importance of respecting each human equally in determining correct action and the ability to generalize our actions (from Kant), and the importance of looking at the consequences of the action on the overall good of the community or group involved (from Mill). Even a full historical complement of the best and the brightest in the tradition doesn't expand the list beyond a relatively small number of philosophers who have been recognized over time, space, and cultures because of the overall adequacy of their theories. The theories are not complementary nor consistent in how they argue that ethical questions should be approached, but they all provide concepts and processes that are useful in thinking through contemporary cases.

From the assistance of the thought of Aristotle, Kant, and Mill, we should consider the following three questions in analyzing cases:

1. Does the intended action respect all persons affected? Does it treat all persons in the situation in a consistent and impartial manner? (from Kant)
2. Is each person getting what he or she is entitled to? Does the intended action tend to promote good overall? Can the agent be helped to understand that his or her individual good comes from promoting the aggregate good of the community? (from Mill)
3. What would your moral hero do? Can you find an alternative that expresses a moderate response rather than an extreme? (from Aristotle)

MIXED FORMALISM

The key to applying classical moral philosophy in the study of practical ethics is to recognize that the different moral theories provide different tools that help us recognize and respond to particular moral features. Sometimes we need to consider how voluntary an action might be or how to avoid extreme reactions. Aristotle can give us a hand here. Or perhaps we need to think carefully about whether a person is being exploited or about what it would mean to be impartial when it is easier not to. Kant is good to consult on these matters. Maybe we need to think about what it means to create aggregate good and how to support the community's interest. Now we want Mill at our side. But all of these questions may arise in the examination of a single case.

Many contemporary philosophers stand on the shoulders of classical philosophers. The contemporary scholars have chosen from the classicists in attempts to create theories that draw on the best of those intuitions as well as their own. Bernard Gert's moral rules theory, for example, is a highly accessible contemporary moral theory for nonphilosophers. I use Gert's theory in my own work in practical ethics and throughout this book, but I have added to his theory. I have credited thought in this work that is purely Gert but have indicated my own expansion of his theory, where appropriate.

Gert is among a large group of contemporary philosophers who draw on a combination of thought from classical theory to create the theories they use today. Sissela Bok is another well-respected contemporary philosopher who uses mixed formalism.

In *Lying: Moral Choice in Public and Private Life*, which is often used in practical ethics discussions on deception, Bok draws upon and includes passages from a number of classical philosophers including Augustine, Thomas Aquinas, Francis Bacon, Hugo Grotius, Immanuel Kant, Henry Sidgwick, R. F. Harrod, Dietrich Bonhoeffer, and G. J. Warnock. But while her sources span centuries of thought, her classification and theorizing about the nature and justification of deception focus on important contemporary issues such as lying in intimate situations, white lies, and lies purportedly for the public good.[7]

THE MORAL COMMUNITY AND
SUBJECTS OF MORAL WORTH

Moral agents are persons who are rational enough to understand the human analogy—they know that other people can be caused harm and that they, themselves, are capable of causing harm to others. According to Gert, "Common morality also includes all those who have been actual moral agents and are still conscious. . . . These actual and former moral agents comprise the smallest group toward which all rational persons agree that morality requires impartiality."[8] Impartiality means that everyone in the group deserves equal moral protections. Because one is a born human being, it follows that it is wrong for others to cause a person harm unless there is a good reason.

While there is disagreement among cultures and among individuals as well about whether to include moral protections for nonviable fetuses and persons in persistent vegetative states, Gert points out that there is substantial agreement regarding infants and children. He says, "It is simply a fact that almost everyone in a technologically advanced society (or a society in which lack of food to sustain life is not a problem) wants to include human infants who will become moral agents in the group toward which the moral rules must be impartially obeyed."[9]

The whole group of those who are determined to be deserving of moral protections equal to one another is called the *moral community*. Every individual within the moral community has equal rights to moral protection. For example, it is not morally permitted for the mother of a child for whom a heart transplant is needed to arrange for the murder of another child to get the needed heart.

The distinction between those within the moral community and those who are not is somewhat arbitrary and has its share of gray areas. Is a baby in the process of being born a member of the moral community or not? Ethically speaking, little distinguishes that baby from the same viable entity it was a day earlier, prior to the beginning of labor. Whether the newborn is a minute out of the birth canal, en route in the birthing process, or still snug in the womb and oblivious to the adventure about to begin, the distinction of place (uterus, birth canal, crib) hardly seems a difference in kind that would justify a morally relevant difference.

Similar questions arise at the other end of life. A person who resides in a persistent vegetative state (PVS) is conventionally treated as having the same moral protections as one who is temporarily unconscious or engaged in a normal night's sleep. PVS patients are not used to donate renewable blood products, for example, although using them as resources for other patients would not harm them. The choice to treat them more like human beings than like corpses is a matter of convention, not a moral or logical implication.

If we limit the moral community[10] to include only persons between birth and death, some scholars conclude that nothing else is worthy of moral consideration. This limitation in moral analysis ignores a class of entities that I call *subjects of moral worth*. Those subjects include, but are not limited to, human fetuses, human corpses, animals, the environment, biosystems, culture, and art.

Subjects of moral worth are not worthy of moral protection equal to that of those within the moral community, but they are worthy of some moral consideration. Subjects of moral worth fill a class that exists between the moral community—those who should be treated impartially in terms of moral protections—and the class of objects that have no intrinsic moral worth, such as empty paper bags.

The first major difference, then, between members of the moral community and other subjects of moral worth is the principle of equality or impartiality. In principle, every person between birth and death is entitled to the same minimal level of moral protection—each person has a right not to be caused pain, death, disability, deprivation of freedom or pleasure without justification.[11] That bad things happen to people without good reason does not provide evidence against the claim that every person has the same moral entitlement. In the past half century, documents such as the Universal Declaration of Human Rights have stated this species-wide moral entitlement clearly, but the idea is not new. Philosophers from the pre-Socratics forward have based their philosophies on the fundamental principle that it is not acceptable to cause harm to other people without good reason.

Subjects of moral worth are not the moral equals of those within the moral community. That is why it is morally permitted for physicians to cause the death of a fetus in order to save the life of the pregnant woman, with the woman's consent.[12] It is important to save works of art, but one would reasonably expect firefighters battling a fire at a museum to carry out living persons first. Thus, protection of a member of the moral community can count as justification for causing harm to something that is merely a subject of moral worth. But what separates subjects of moral worth from entities not entitled to moral consideration at all is the fact that if something is a subject of moral worth, then there is some harm that it should not be caused without justification.

What is owed to a subject of moral worth is, first, identical to that which is owed to a member of the moral community—do not cause harm without justification. However, what counts as a harm for a subject of moral worth is often different from what counts as a harm for those in the moral community.

Universal direct harms for members of the moral community include death, pain, disability, deprivation of opportunity, and deprivation of pleasure.[13] It is ethically prohibited to cause a member of the moral community to suffer any of these harms without adequate justification. The human analogy serves as the basis for believing that all people can suffer these harms.

On the other hand, not all subjects of moral worth can suffer all of these direct harms. What counts as harmful for subjects of moral worth will differ subject to subject.

The harms that can inarguably be caused to a viable fetus or sentient animal, for example, are the harms of physical pain and psychological distress. What makes pain and distress harms to sentient creatures is their ability to perceive noxious stimuli. However, unlike pain and distress, painless death may not be a harm for a human fetus or for a nonhuman animal that does not contemplate its past or future. Being deprived of opportunity is not harmful for a being that cannot anticipate that opportunity.

Harms that can be caused to the natural environment or wildlife include disruption of the biosystem upon which sustainability depends.

Harms caused to objects of culture include the destruction of the intergenerational memory that culture preserves.

Harms caused to human corpses include desecration that holds the memory of the once living person up to ridicule or lack of respect.

Generally speaking, harm for a subject of moral worth is something that destroys or threatens to destroy the aspect of the entity that gives it value.

A third difference between obligations toward human beings and subjects of moral worth is that while every rational person has an obligation to avoid causing other humans unjustified harm, subjects of moral worth have, instead, some people with special *stewardship* obligations to protect them.

For example, I use a service dog and thus have special obligations toward that subject of moral worth. My obligation is to protect her from the new harms that she faces in the process of doing her work for me. It would be wrong for strangers to go out of their way to step on my dog's feet, but it is my responsibility, not theirs, to keep the dog out of harm's way.

Art gallery directors have special stewardship obligations to protect the art under their care. The average person has no moral responsibility to know that one piece is an object of art and another is a three-year-old's scrawl.

Thus, there is no obligation for people to act *impartially* toward subjects of moral worth. Instead, people in general must depend upon the stewards of subjects of moral worth to protect these subjects from the harms they can be caused. Lacking the human analogy that makes minimal obligations toward other human beings easy to understand, stewards also have the special role of educating other humans about the nature of the subjects over which they have stewardship.

An understanding of subjects of moral worth provides an additional question to analyze:

4. Are there subjects of moral worth who should be considered in this situation?

SOME FEMINIST INFLUENCES

Women have provided philosophical contributions as long as men have, but historically, their work was ignored or not given the same degree of status or consideration. Historical and contemporary thought by women philosophers represents at least as diverse a range of thought as does the Western male tradition, but just as one can find agreement among Western philosophers regarding the fundamental moral unit, universality, and avoidance of harms, one can see similarities across the critiques of traditional Western philosophy that are offered by some contemporary feminist theorists. For example, philosopher Virginia Held summarizes the critiques of male bias in the history of ethics in three ways: "1) the split between reason and emotion and the devaluation of emotion; 2) the public/private distinction and the relegation of the private to the natural; and 3) the concept of the self as constructed from a male point of view."[14] Feminist theorists have addressed those biases in different ways, but these basic criticisms suggest additional considerations for moral relevancy.

Some feminist philosophers, for example, have provided an alternative to the Western classical assumption of the individual person as the *fundamental moral unit* for analysis. If, as some women philosophers have argued, the relationship between people is considered the fundamental moral unit, ethical analysis changes. Instead of finding solutions that protect everyone's individual rights, solutions are proposed that best allow for relationships to continue. Relationships rarely include individuals with equal power, status, and abilities. Relational ethics therefore may require solutions that address the needs of the most vulnerable. Relationships exist among people who are connected, so the language of how people should act toward one another may be very different from a language that starts with one's obligations to not interfere with the rights of strangers.

Aristotle's ethics, upon which so much of our Western democratic public policy rests, is an ethics of strangers. It is a guidebook for how to act in regard to others, no matter who they might be. It rests on the assumption that the people who make ethical choices are those who are free, competent, and powerful in ways equivalent to one another. The Western philosophical tradition was generally silent regarding people and experiences that took place in the private family sphere rather than the public state sphere.[15] And the experience of private space with people of different ages and different needs is different, indeed, from the public space traditionally inhabited by free men. As philosopher Rosemarie Tong points out, "Women *listen* to the babbling of babies, the prattling of teens, and the reminiscences of the old, while men *speak* to each other about business matters, public policies, and professional affairs."[16]

When Aristotle addressed issues of friendship or family relationships, it was in relation to how these connections helped the individual reach telios, or self-actualization. Relationships were viewed as instrumental to individual fulfillment. For example, Aristotle tells us that "if the function of a friend is to do good rather than to be treated well, if the performance of good deeds is the mark of a good man and of excellence, and if it is nobler to do good to a friend than to a stranger, then a man of high moral standards will need people to whom he can do good."[17] Friendship is important in only an instrumental sense, and in Aristotle's theory, women reach their telios by serving men.

An alternative view of relationships, found in the writing of some feminist theories, is to view relationships as intrinsically worthwhile and important to sustain in their own right. Referring to psychologist Carol Gilligan, who differentiated female approaches to moral reasoning from male approaches, philosopher Annette C. Baier says, "Gilligan's girls and women saw morality as a matter of preserving valued ties to others, of preserving the conditions for their care and mutual care."[18] Philosopher Nel Noddings argues that human beings are defined by their connections when they talk about themselves and others. She contends that caring is a relational value that belongs to the connection itself rather than to individuals.[19] An individual can't be said to be "caring" unless there is another person or a subject of moral worth in the equation. One cares for someone or something.

Western moral theories have focused on civic life rather than family and friends. Those theories and contemporary policy and practice all favor productive success in society over reproductive success. Consider the difference in financial reward for occupations that promote the productive arts, such as manufacture and investment, and those that promote the reproductive arts, such as child care and housecleaning. In school, children are primarily taught skills that will make them successful in the workplace; the number of hours of formal instruction on how to be good friends, good partners, and good parents are nonexistent in comparison.

The rational, autonomous human being has been the primary focus in traditional Western philosophy. The result is that 2000 years of moral theorizing have prioritized values of rights, autonomy, and noninterference. Relationships among strangers are viewed as a mathematical puzzle: consideration of what constitutes fair distribution of goods, with discussion of reciprocal exchange.

The minimal expectation that pervades Western moral philosophy is an obligation to avoid harming one another. The primary disagreements have been over what counts as harm, when one should be held accountable, and what counts as adequate justification for causing harm.

The language of Western moral philosophy is a language of separateness and conflict. Putting together conclusions and reasons is building an "argument." Responses to those connections are "counterarguments." The best arguments are those that can be "defended" against objections.

However, as some feminist theorists have pointed out, no one starts out as a rational, autonomous human being. We all start out as fetuses dependent on a gestating mother for life itself. Once born, each child is utterly dependent on a caretaker.

An ethical theory that grows out of caretaking is more likely to be based on interdependency and on the needs of, rather than the freedoms of, individuals.

If these feminist perspectives had been historically fundamental, classical moral theory might look very different. Instead of resting analysis on an overarching principle that all individuals have equal rights, conclusions would appeal to the difference in the needs of particular persons. Instead of worrying about how each person's liberty can be best protected, ethical theory would ask which actions might best preserve relationships among people and provide care for those in need.

Analysis itself might sound different. Instead of conflict of rights, we might consider a confluence of needs. Instead of argument, we might have deliberation. Instead of defending an argument that can withstand attack, we might find ourselves thinking together about how each person involved could get what he or she really needs.

Just as mixed formalism allows us to take the best from the classical male philosophers, a mixed formalist approach allows for the use of feminist thought as well. So, we now add the following question to our mix:

5. Is each person in the situation getting what he or she needs? How can we devise a solution that addresses each person's needs, and most particularly, the needs of the most vulnerable? Does the intended action promote relationship, and does it promote community? Does it promote trust among people? Is the process of decision making itself respectful of everyone involved?

There are other alternatives to classical Western moral philosophy. Some, such as Eastern and indigenous approaches, were well established before Western thought was recorded. Many theoretical tools can fit into the practical ethics kit. The broader the variety of tools, the more flexible the practitioner will be in analyzing alternative aspects and actions within real-life situations. Chapter 7 addresses some differences between indigenous and Western thought.

To return to the case that opened this chapter, seminar participants have discussed how Thomas might have approached this situation if he had been more secure in his understanding of classical philosophy and if he had been clear about what he hoped to achieve in terms of his teaching objectives. What follows is a composite of the best of those discussions.

After reading the case, Thomas asked students to bring a philosophical perspective into the conversation. "Don't tell me what you think Sara should do. Don't even tell me what some philosopher might say was the right thing for Sara to do," he said. "I want you to think about the case without specifically looking for a solution. If Aristotle, Kant, Mill, or our feminist philosophers were observing the scene, just tell me what you think they might observe about the situation in which Sara found herself."

The students were silent for a few minutes while they struggled with this new way of approaching casework.

"It seems to me," said Dawn, "that Aristotle would say that Sara is trying to be a self-actualized person, to reach her own telios by extending herself beyond what it means to be doing her job. She is kind of like a moral hero, operating out a theory of virtues."

"But that's not all that Aristotle says," Rachel countered. "The person of practical wisdom is not someone who acts in extremes. She should be trying to find the Golden Mean."

"Interesting points," Thomas said, acknowledging both students and reviewing the Aristotelian notions the students had mentioned. "You are both right. Aristotle tells us to look to the person of practical wisdom for guidance. He also tells us that the person of practical wisdom chooses a moderate path—the virtue of moderation—which will be the mean between the vice of excess and the vice of deficiency. Let's try that type of reasoning here. What would the extremes look like for Sara or another journalist in her situation?"

Silence again while the students thought about vices of excess and deficiency for Sara in her struggle to do a good job.

"Well, it would be wrong for her to just do what she had to do to keep her job and not care about the people she writes about," John offered. "And, it would be equally wrong for her to try to do everyone else's job by taking care of all people in need," added Matt. "As Sara leans toward that direction, she should be especially careful about following that path."

Rachel's face brightened as she listened to this analysis. "I just thought of something weird. It's like the feminists we read might agree with Aristotle on this one. Matt is saying that Sara should not sacrifice herself for everyone even if she doesn't realize that being on the job 24-7 isn't good for her or for anyone else. That's an extreme. Sara is not the first woman to think that the best way to excel is by sacrificing herself and doing more than anyone else. Her boss and union representative may be paternalistic, but I don't think that her willingness to have her life consumed by her job makes her a moral hero. I don't think that is a good model for young journalists to follow."

Thomas noticed that the class time was just about up. "We'll pick this up next class," he said, "but your written assignment is to take what you have learned from philosophical theory to think more about this case. Think of Sara, the city editor, the union representative, and all the other journalists in the newsroom as persons who have a stake here. There are other actors, of course: the story subjects and those who work for the social agencies in town. So, you can also think about the situation as a community-wide issue.

"Your job is to bring philosophical wisdom into a discussion of the case. That just happened when we started talking about Aristotle and feminist responses. You may find that the philosophers agree more than they disagree, but maybe for different reasons. Use your philosophical knowledge to clarify

the morally relevant issues rather than to look for a solution. There may be a range of morally permissible solutions, but for right now, let's try to use the great thoughts of all the philosophers in figuring out how to articulate the problem."

Thomas didn't know exactly what to expect from the students' individual work, but he knew the assignment would provide the start to some wonderful interaction in the next class. "Who knows," he thought, "they may even come up with some ideas that will work for them when they find themselves in their first jobs."

NOTES

1. The notion of rationality used here is from contemporary philosopher Bernard Gert. A careful description of what is meant by rationality and irrationality can be found in Bernard Gert, *Morality: Its Nature and Justification* (New York: Oxford University Press, 2005), 29–55.

2. Gert, *Morality*, 30.

3. This is not to suggest that only adult humans are capable of rational acts. If we consider rationality as the ability to know and avoid harms, other beings and children are capable of those acts. Moral agency is connected with rationality in that one should be held accountable only for those acts that one is able to comprehend as causing something that another would want to avoid. For example, I know that my older golden retriever wants to avoid having her food eaten by the younger dog. She also knows that the younger dog wishes to avoid having her food eaten. I am therefore justified in correcting the older dog when, upon finishing her meal, she pushes the younger dog away to grab an extra bite or two. The older dog is rational to the extent that she knows she wants to avoid the harm of having her food eaten, knows that the younger dog is like her in this way, and can choose to avoid eating the other dog's food. Whether this is a *moral* choice on the part of the older dog is a subject for another book.

4. See Peter Suber, "Stages of Argument," www.earlham.edu/~peters/courses/arg stages.htm (accessed April 24, 2005) for an excellent explanation of the need for cogency and strength in developing arguments for ethics.

5. Gert, *Morality*, 4–5.

6. See Immanuel Kant, *Lectures on Ethics*, trans. Louis Infield (Indianapolis, IN: Hackett, 1980).

7. Sissela Bok, *Lying: Moral Choice in Public and Private Life* (New York: Vintage, 1978).

8. Gert, *Morality*, 142.

9. Gert, *Morality*, 143.

10. Logically speaking, one cannot broaden the group to which one impartially applies equal moral protections unless it is possible, in principle, to provide protections for those new members that are equal to everyone already in the group. Therefore, it is not logical to suggest, for example, that white-tailed deer be included in the moral community. We can imagine what it would be like to protect all born human beings from being caused

intentional harm, even if that is not likely to happen in our lifetimes. All we need to do is imagine a democratic world government, population control, food supply sufficient for the population, and a lack of terrorism. However, protecting all white-tailed deer would mean, in my Montana backyard, depriving mountain lions and wolves of their dinner. Even in principle, one cannot imagine what it would mean to provide protection for one species of wild animal equal to what we provide for those in the moral community. Even if we know that some people are treated badly, we know that it would be possible for the bad treatment not to occur. Other people would survive if all people were protected from harm. This is not the case if a species of wild animal were equally protected. Other wild animals would be deprived of the food they need to survive. See Gert, *Morality*, 145–148 for more on the nature of moral community.

11. Gert, *Morality*, 159–186.

12. However, it is also rational for a pregnant woman to choose her own death over the death of her viable fetus. A member of the moral community may consider the protection of a subject of moral worth as a good enough reason to consent to the personal suffering of harms. But it is morally prohibited for others to place the interests of a subject of moral worth over the interests of a member of the moral community without the consent of the person who will have harm inflicted upon him or her.

13. Gert, *Morality*, 159–186.

14. Virginia Held, "Feminist Transformations of Moral Theory," *Philosophy and Phenomenological Research* (Fall 1990): 60–64.

15. Aristotle does address relationships such as friendships and relationships among people who are not considered "equals" (such as husband-wife, parent-child, owner-slave), but this an adjunct to his more general moral theory.

16. Rosemarie Tong, *Feminine and Feminist Ethics* (Belmont, CA: Wadsworth, 1993), 6.

17. Aristotle, *Nicomachean Ethics*, trans. Martin Ostwald (Upper Saddle River, NJ: Prentice Hall, 1999), 263.

18. Annette C. Baier, "What Do Women Want in a Moral Theory?" *Nous* 19, no. 1 (1985): 31.

19. Tong, *Feminine and Feminist Ethics*, 115.

Chapter Five

Relativism and Moral Development

THE PROBLEM OF FATALISTIC RELATIVISM

Fatalistic relativism: It's as common as case studies in practical ethics discussions. For example, a professor presents a complex case and then asks, "Was Bob's action ethical?" Students shift uncomfortably. One finally says, "It's not my business to judge him."

That's fatalistic relativism.

In small group discussion, a student explains why she believes the death penalty is morally prohibited. "What do you think?" she asks the other group members. "What's right for you is right for you," another student shrugs.

That's fatalistic relativism.

Fatalistic relativism is characterized by an unwillingness to make moral judgments. It should not be confused with philosophical theories of relativism. Those philosophical theories stand in contrast to universal theories. Universal theories claim that there are moral rules or principles that extend across culture and time. Relativistic theories argue that what's right or wrong varies between cultures or over centuries.

Fatalistic relativism is a default position people take when they resist engaging in moral analysis or when they don't feel safe enough to take the intellectual risk necessary to do so. Fatalistic relativism denies the normative quality of ethics discussion.

Thinking one's way out of an ethical problem is hard work for everyone. Professionals tend to avoid moral analysis by relabeling ethical problems as clinical problems or editorial problems or management problems.

They avoid moral analysis by substituting legal thinking, saying, "There is nothing illegal about what I intend to do."

Or they substitute economic thinking by saying, "My decision is good for business."

Or they substitute description for moral judgment, saying that it doesn't matter what people *should* do, they're going to do what they want to do anyway.

All decisions involving humans or subjects of moral worth have ethical aspects. Yet few people start the morning thinking they will have continuing ethical responsibility as they proceed through their day. It is far easier to believe there are no ethical concerns until a problem arises, it is labeled as an ethical problem, and potential blameworthiness is established. Being ethically aware is hard work.

Sometimes people seem stuck in their inability to make moral judgments. Fatalistic relativism is a transitional period between stages of moral development. As with all stages of growth, progress in ethical thinking and action cannot be demanded, it can only be encouraged. As is the case with all development, people will regress when threatened, and people who are capable of the most sophisticated level of analysis and behavior will opt for less sophisticated levels some of the time. No one can force someone else to be at a different level of development from where that person happens to be; yet all of us can help others stretch beyond their current stages. That stretching, however, is possible only in environments that make it safe to take risk.

This chapter unites moral development and ethics education. Those new to the topics may think that the connection is self-evident. However, in the 1970s and 1980s, scholars expressed discomfort that the teaching of ethics might lead to moral development.

In *Ethics Teaching in Higher Education*, Daniel Callahan states, "The purpose of an ethics course—that of critical inquiry—would be begged by a pre-established blueprint of what will count as acceptable moral behavior."[1] The book's summary reminds readers, "Courses in ethics ought not explicitly seek behavioral change in students."[2]

While making people good is not an appropriate instructional objective, we are all in a period of moral growth and development that runs from birth to death. It would be odd if study of ethical decision making did not stimulate participants to more sophisticated self-examination. The Hastings Center's goals themselves depend on high levels of moral development for achievement. Goal 3, for example, "eliciting a sense of moral obligation," assumes an agent's understanding that one is accountable for his or her voluntary actions. Goal 5, "tolerating—and reducing—disagreement and ambiguity," requires that the agent be able to recognize others' perspectives as potentially valid in the face of one's opposing view and that the agent can develop a method for choosing among recognized alternatives. Both of these goals require that agents have attained a high level of moral sophistication.

Learning practical ethics—if that is meant to imply that students develop a more sophisticated way of dealing with ethical issues than they had at the beginning of the term—can only be accomplished as students' moral development occurs through ethics education.

ELEMENTS OF MORAL DEVELOPMENT THEORIES

Moral development theories rest on the notion that human beings develop morally in a way that is analogous with how humans develop physically, cognitively, and linguistically. Just as a baby must acquire reciprocal leg motion before she can walk, all people must feel they can protect themselves before they can take others' needs into consideration. They must be able to understand what external authority means by "good" and "bad" before they can evaluate the appropriateness of the external rules for themselves.

Moral development depends on a number of starting assumptions:

- The universality of some human values
- Sequential progression that is not static
- Recognition of environment as a variable in development
- A definition of moral sophistication

Universality

Adequate moral development theories, like adequate ethical theories, *describe* the way that people grow as well as *prescribe* the best direction for development. The description of moral sophistication offered should be consistently descriptive across culture and time.

As communication scholar Michael Traber explains,

> The evidence . . . demonstrates that certain ethical proto-norms—above all, truth telling, commitment to justice, freedom in solidarity, and respect for human dignity—are validated as core values in . . . different cultures. These values are called universal not just because they hold true cross-culturally; in fact, there may be cultures or there might be future cultures where such evidence is spurious. The universality of these values is beyond culture. It is rooted ontologically in the nature of human beings. It is by virtue of what it means to be human that these values are universal.[3]

By way of example, the Universal Declaration of Human Rights embraces what Traber refers to as core values. We would not label some actions as "violations" of human rights unless we knew those actions to be wrong.

Thus, the universality requirement of moral development theories rests on the belief that with the right environment and stimulus, humans have the potential to grow toward an appreciation of ethical proto-norms.

An adequate theory of moral development extends across cultures, as does an adequate theory of linguistic development. An adequate linguistic theory will describe how children learn to speak their native language, regardless of whether the child is learning to speak Arabic or Russian. How a person comes to choose to behave well toward others should be adequately described by a moral development theory, regardless of where that person grows up.

However, just as various factors impede physical, or linguistic, or cognitive development, the same is true for moral development.

James Q. Wilson reflects on the human "moral sense":

> To say that people have a moral sense is not the same thing as saying that they are innately good. A moral sense must compete with other senses that are natural to humans—the desire to survive, acquire possessions, indulge in sex, or accumulate power—in short, with self-interest narrowly defined. How that struggle is resolved will differ depending on character, our circumstances, and the cultural and political tendencies of the day. But saying that a moral sense exists is the same thing as saying that humans, by their nature, are potentially good.[4]

Sequential Progression without Static Stages

All moral development theories include a notion of *sequential progression* that includes a move from focus on self to focus on others in addition to self. People grow from a *heteronomous* stance, in which right and wrong are defined externally, to an *autonomous* stance, in which right and wrong are determined internally. Autonomy means that the morally mature person has internalized values and is able to use personal judgment, rather than the opinions of others, in determining how to act and in explaining the reasons for action.

Moral development, like other kinds of development, allows for regression and depends on a person's achievement of one series of abilities before moving on to another. To continue with the analogy of linguistic progression, a child must babble combinations of consonants and syllables before she will be able to articulate full sentences. However, when she can articulate full sentences, she may still utter single words to express herself.

Like linguistic or physical development, moral sophistication is not something one attains and keeps in some saintly way. It is more like a degree of fluency. Even the most sophisticated among us make grammatical mistakes or choose to speak in less sophisticated ways than we are capable.

I believe I have reached a reasonably high level of moral sophistication (but then, who doesn't?). But if I were driving down the road and noticed a police car behind me with lights flashing and siren wailing, I would pull over immediately. I would stop because I would be fearful of greater punishment if I didn't. I would stop because I felt helpless to do otherwise. I would stop in subjection to the authority of the state. All three of these reasons are indicative of using reasoning from a low level of moral development.

Despite what might seem as morally primitive reasoning, pulling over to the side of the road for the reasons that I offer is far more rational than if I were to act in what moral theorists would call a sophisticated, autonomous way. Autonomous action would require me to contemplate a variety of important issues, with police in pursuit. I should consider the social benefit of my stopping and think about whether it is really my moral duty, rather than simply my legal duty, to stop. I would need to consider whether my stopping in response to the threat of police action promotes a way for all our needs to be met in a nonviolent, nonconflicted way.

In short, by the time I considered alternative actions in a morally sophisticated way, I would have attracted the attention of the entire highway patrol. My refusal to submit to heteronomous expectations would guarantee me plenty of time to autonomously contemplate these issues while I sat in jail.

Even for those with a sophisticated use of the language, there are times when yelling, "Help!" or "Fire!" or "Rape!" is more appropriate than developing a treatise that contextually explains the situation, describes alternative responses, and argues for a preferred reaction. Moral sophistication means that the individual has a wide range of reasoning ability in determining how to act. It does not imply that the most complicated or sophisticated choice is always best.

However, lower developmental stages *limit* a person's alternatives for thought and action. By analogy, a young speaker will not be able to duplicate or explain the rhetorical moves of a sportscaster or talk show host. A beginning tennis player cannot duplicate the moves of a top player.

It is easy to see the limitations of less sophisticated discussants in ethics discussions. Some participants may feel bored or frustrated if the discussion is happening at a level requiring an ability to consider concepts that are still beyond them. How often I have watched some students engage in complex analysis of whether a potential action appropriately respects the rights of all involved and then see another student bring the discussion to a halt by claiming, "People just do what they want to further their own interests." The second student has not reached a level of sophistication needed to understand agents who would put everyone's needs, including their own, at the same level of consideration.

Empirical work on moral development has shown[5] that people can see the adequacy of stages that are slightly above their own, but not more than that. An appropriate classroom response to the student unable to understand the rights-level discussion is "So, you're saying that people always act in a way that benefits themselves. Can you think of any exceptions to this rule?" The student himself, or others, will certainly be able to provide examples of people putting themselves at risk for the benefit of another. Of course, the student may respond that the actor is *really* doing what will ultimately make *him* feel good, but at least the student has been exposed to an alternative. Examining alternatives is necessary for moral growth.

Moral development happens within one's own personal development but also within the context of one's professional development. A young doctor or journalist or lawyer will retreat to a low level of moral development when trying to determine how to act within her new environment and profession. At first, she will need to figure out the external demands on her and will appropriately respond to her authorities and peers. Once the person feels safe within the environment, her general moral developmental level achieved will become more evident. But it is not surprising to find that a person may be able to reason and act at a much higher stage of development in some areas of life than in others. The ability to integrate, rather than compartmentalize, all of one's varied life experiences requires conscious effort and a high level of moral sophistication.

Environment

Environments encourage or discourage moral growth and development. Development of any kind beyond a rudimentary level is dependent upon which capacities are encouraged and which are discouraged.

The dependency on environment and opportunity for growth is not unique to moral development. Developing athletic or musical proficiency requires attention and practice. Linguistic excellence doesn't come naturally, although the ability to speak does. In an analogous way, moral excellence requires training and encouragement beyond a conventional level. It is consistent with development theories to find persons or groups within society who lack the ability to communicate beyond the most rudimentary level, who fall far short of norms for physical fitness, or whose moral reasoning is at a preconventional level. A person may have the capacity to achieve a high level of development yet never attain that level. And he certainly will mature differently in an environment that favors one sort of development over another.

Moral Sophistication

While many scholars have noted points on a continuum from reasoning in a morally primitive way to reasoning in a morally sophisticated way,[6] I focus here on the work of Lawrence Kohlberg, Carol Gilligan, and William Perry. These three moral development theorists provide an integrative set of notions of moral development that fits particularly well for adults who are analyzing their own motivations and the reasoning behind the actions of others. These scholars provide different, but complementary, ways of examining moral growth and development.

Kohlberg fits his conception of moral development into the Western philosophical rights-based system. His highest stage[7] of moral sophistication mirrors the orientation of eighteenth-century German philosopher Immanuel Kant and twentieth-century American philosopher John Rawls. People who have become morally sophisticated try to meet their role-related responsibilities, don't grant themselves special privileges, don't intrude on the rights of others, and recognize the integrity of all other individuals.

Gilligan sees the morally mature person as championing the needs of the vulnerable and making decisions with the priority of sustaining relationships among people.

Perry tracks yet a different notion of development by noting moral maturity as the ability of people to take stands that express their beliefs while, at the same time, recognizing that new understandings may change what they believe.

The three theories are complementary in that they explain different, but equally essential, aspects of becoming a morally sophisticated decision maker.

Kohlberg's Theory

Lawrence Kohlberg,[8] who began his work in moral development with his dissertation in 1955 and ended his career as a Harvard professor and psychologist with his death in January 1987, advanced the moral development theory of Jean Piaget. Piaget, a developmental psychologist, recognized that children used a progressively more sophisticated manner of moral reasoning that complemented their intellectual and cognitive development.[9]

Kohlberg demonstrated through empirical studies that individuals developed understandings by progressing through six stages of personal development that could be classified within three evolving societal perspectives.

The first level of development, the preconventional level, attaches judgments of right and wrong to the fear of punishment and hope for reward. People who find themselves in a foreign and potentially dangerous environment will first determine how to avoid punishment or noxious consequences. That is stage one. Once they realize how to stay out of trouble, they will use stage-two thinking to figure out how to bring about good consequences for themselves.

The conventional level that follows, so called because it is the level to which most people progress and within which almost all of us usually operate, is still heteronomous—dependent on external factors for judging right and wrong—but is social in a way that the preconventional stages are not. Rather than care simply about personal pain or pleasure, the person using stage-three thinking chooses to do what will bring about the approval of others. The next stage within this level is adherence to laws, norms, codes, or other rules. When using stage-four reasoning, the person reasons that the best way to get along and for the group to function effectively is if all people know the rules and follow them. So while people using stage-three reasoning are subject to the whims of their peers, people who have attained stage-four reasoning will think that it is the moral responsibility of all persons to learn and follow relevant rules.

Postconventional thinking requires people to step outside societal expectations and examine norms and expectations in a broader context. One indicator that people are able to reason at the initial postconventional stage of reasoning is that they are able to make choices using a utilitarian perspective of justice. Is everyone getting what he or she deserves? If so, then the right thing to do, for someone using stage-five reasoning, is that which will bring about the greatest overall benefit to the group at hand. With stage-six reasoning, people make decisions from the understanding that it is essential to treat each individual as an end in himself or herself, with rights equal to all others, as the ultimate way of ensuring justice. Justice includes individuals getting what they deserve and a fair distribution of community goods.

The different stages are not necessarily in conflict with one another. There is nothing wrong with feeling pleasure at being awarded the Nobel Peace Prize for having improved the human condition.

Gilligan's Theory

Carol Gilligan, a colleague of Kohlberg, argues[10] that Kohlberg's scope of morality is incomplete, both conceptually and empirically. Conceptually, Kohlberg's developmental scale is based on a notion of rights and equity. Gilligan describes a complementary theory that illustrates the development of a person's ability to care, which she argues is an equally essential part of the moral sphere. Gilligan provides a developmental scheme that contains "the language of responsibilities that sustains connection."[11]

While Kohlberg's theory developed out of longitudinal studies of boys and men, Gilligan focused her efforts on how girls and women develop their abilities to make ethical decisions. Without arguing for either a biological or sociological cause, Gilligan demonstrates that the women she studied developed morally more from a caretaking perspective than from a perspective of coming to respect individual rights and autonomy.

The developmental sequence in Gilligan's theory progresses from the need to protect what one perceives as a powerless self, to believing that the right thing to do is to care for others, to a final mature level of integrating the care for self with the care for others.[12]

Unlike Kohlberg's focus on "how do I get what I have a right to get?" the question that Gilligan's young or novice decision maker asks is "how do I protect myself from all those more powerful people?" Those preconventional strategies include seeking to please powerful others who are in a position to cause harm to the more vulnerable person.

The growing decision maker then begins to recognize herself as a person of power, a person who can affect the environment around her. At this level, equivalent to Kohlberg's conventional level, the person no longer sees the ultimate good as protecting herself in a chaotic world but sees the good in seizing the power she does have in order to care for others. Mid-twentieth-century popular culture presented the morally ideal wife and mother as the woman who sacrificed herself for the good of her husband and children. Her effectiveness, her goodness, was evaluated on the basis of how well her family fared. This mythical woman was reflecting Gilligan's level of reasoning from a perspective of self-sacrifice.

For those advancing to a postconventional stage, the long, hard struggles of needing to care for one's self and needing to care for others merge in the realization that it is possible for everyone's needs to be met. Caring for all becomes a goal that includes the needs and legitimate desires of the self on equal footing with the needs and legitimate desires of others. The best moral decisions are those that take care of everyone's needs. If everyone's needs can't be met, then the most vulnerable people in the situation take priority.

Gilligan's empirical work allowed for the voices of women to be considered in mapping moral development, but her conclusion was not that women are different moral beings from men. According to Gilligan, the integrated, morally mature person would exhibit both types of development:

> To understand how the tension between responsibilities and rights sustains the dialectic of human development is to see the integrity of two disparate modes of experience that are in the end connected. While an ethic of justice proceeds from the premise of equality—that everyone should be treated the same—an ethic of care rests on the premise of nonviolence—that no one should be hurt. In the representation of maturity, both perspectives converge in the realization that just as inequality

adversely affects both parties in an unequal relationship, so too violence is destruc-
tive for everyone involved.[13]

Perry's Theory

William Perry,[14] who died in 1998, was a Harvard professor of developmental
psychology and education. He connected the moral development of college
students to their beliefs about the nature of knowledge. He postulated, and
provided empirical studies to demonstrate, that persons move through a series
of "positions" in their quest to understand the basis of knowledge and the
role that authority plays in determining right action. Those positions are
delineated by three major markers: dualism, relativism, and commitment with
uncertainty.

Dualism rests on the belief that there are accessible right and wrong
answers. People using this stage of reasoning see their task as that of finding
the right authorities who can provide the right answers. Good authority figures are those who are perceived as providing the truth. The search for the
truth crosses the realms of factual knowledge of the world as well as ethics.

When the person realizes that authorities, even good authorities, disagree,
he moves to a position of multiplicity. The individual may give up on the idea
that anything is objectively "true." Here, the person realizes that, along with
"right" answers and "wrong" answers, there are many questions for which
the answers are not yet known, or perhaps will never be known. At this point,
he moves from reliance on authority to provide the right answer to a dawning
awareness that no one may ever know for sure what is right.

Relativism marks the style of reasoning in which people have given up the
idea that authority has the right answer. The belief of someone reasoning in
this way is that knowledge and moral concepts are contextual. People may
agree on methods of inquiry, but these methods cannot be expected to provide an objectively true outcome. Someone moving to a more advanced style
of reasoning will recognize that some reasons for holding an opinion are better than others.

Through education and experience, individuals reach the stage in which
they can make commitments with uncertainty. Now they are able to integrate
what seems to be true with their own reflection and analysis of the authority
upon which it is based. The person thinks, "I understand that something may
happen to shake my belief, but now this is what I think is right. I'm willing
to act on that belief because I can justify it to myself and others."

Reflection on one's own growth, development, and fluctuation between the
stages calls to mind examples of how the three theories complement one
another. When one feels powerless, it is natural to look to authority for

answers and for reward. Strong identification with peers or a social group encourages tolerance for perspectives of others in the group, a desire to please others, and a tendency to develop "group think." Owning and standing up for one's own beliefs requires the willingness to offer justification beyond conventional thinking.

An Example of Perry's Theory Applied to Ethics Instruction

Professors cannot insist that students be able to make, embrace, and defend a normative stance—which is that later Perry position of commitment with uncertainty—until the students have worked their way through the earlier stages.

A few freshmen have worked through to a committed, but not dogmatic, view of knowledge and of morality by the time they enter college. On the other hand, some seniors graduate still hoping to hear some authority's right answer. But the majority of students move through Perry positions during their college experience, beginning with the seeking of authoritative answers and ending with comfort in taking a stand despite uncertainty. Most college professors have different expectations for freshmen than they have for their graduating seniors. Without explicit knowledge of developmental theory, good teachers unconsciously adjust their teaching to their students' developmental levels.

Courses geared to freshmen or sophomores are best designed with clear structure and expectations. Structure creates a safe place for students who are just beginning to struggle with a multiplicity of answers.

Rarely will I ask students at this stage what *they* believe about something, except to get the conversation started. Instead, from readings—use of authority—I ask students to construct the arguments they find there. I ask them to examine the reasons that are offered for various conclusions found in text. I ask them which premises seem strongest, which seem weakest, and why. I always include "so-and-so says so" as a premise and rejoice when that premise gets quickly dumped as not providing sufficient reason for holding a belief.

Relativism, the next stage in the Perry progression, is a stage that I struggle against in myself and with my students. In my own quest for knowledge and determination of what counts as morally ideal action, I seek universal answers I can hold on to, at least for a time. My personal psychological comfort rests on my ability to appeal to principle and apply that principle to specific situations. Therefore, I feel frustrated and threatened by stubborn student relativists. They refuse to make normative judgments. The more I insist that they structure normative arguments, the more they resist doing so. It is personally difficult for me to celebrate students' relativism as a stage in their personal growth and current reasoning style when I just want them to get over it.

My personal challenge is to get beyond my own difficulties in dealing with students who are at this stage. When I am at my best, I say to them, "Can you believe how many different ways people approach things? Let's see if we can list all the different cultural views on this particular topic."

I provide alternative views and approaches from which to choose. I use their own relativistic views as an opening for introducing concepts of diversity and multiculturalism. If they are going to be stubbornly focused on eschewing universal value, the least I can do is help them learn to theorize well about differences. I work to move students in this stage from relativism toward pluralism.

I ask students to look for elements of agreement among different opinions and introduce the notions of moral permissibility, morally ideal behavior, and moral prohibition. There may be vast disagreement among cultures, and even within the class, about what is the *best* thing to do in a particular situation. But there will be lots of agreement about what is the *wrong* thing to do. The concepts of moral permissibility, morally ideal behavior, and moral prohibition expand the ethics discussion beyond a dualistic right and wrong to one that accepts a multiplicity of answers. But even that multiplicity has limits.

When I return papers to the class, I say, "Isn't it interesting that the students who got As each wrote very different essays and still got the same good grade? How is that possible? What common standards do you think that I express in the grading?"

The Platonic dialogue *Gorgias* is an adventure for relativists. They delight in Socrates' process of negative questioning as a way of poking holes in commonly held beliefs. At an earlier, dualistic stage, students who are still hoping that authority will provide the one *right* answer perceive Socrates' technique as manipulative and disrespectful. Dualistic participants are frustrated when Socrates criticizes beliefs without offering an alternative. Once students have reached the relativistic level, they are less troubled when Socrates and his discussants fail to come to agreement.

As students progress from relativism to commitment with uncertainty, professors can become their students' mentors. Mentoring students who are ready to do their own independent thinking is a role different from being the students' safe authority figure or their guide through a world of different opinions. At this stage, I respect the students' ability to come to their own well-considered normative decisions. But even at this senior, graduate, or adult-learner level, I don't expect them to put it all together on their own.

In graduate, professional, and a few upper-level undergraduate settings, I develop assignments that allow advanced students to practice analytic skills after building a foundation of less risky activity. For example, I like to assign an extensive case analysis to be written in three parts, over the course of the full semester.

Part I of the paper asks students to identify the ethical issue to be examined and to come to an understanding of what various authorities say about the topic. Known as a problem statement and literature review in scholarly circles, part I mirrors the dualistic position of getting clear about what authorities have to say and identifying areas where authorities may disagree.

Part II of the paper asks students to research and find out as much as they can about the perceived facts of the matter. This mimics the move into relativism. Students are expected to talk to individuals involved in an ethically charged issue[15] and examine primary documents so they can understand and honestly reflect as many perspectives relating to a case or issue as possible. This part of the assignment is always easiest for the student who starts out his or her research without a clear conclusion or judgment. Students who begin the paper thinking they know their conclusion have a much harder time in honestly presenting different points of view. A test of whether a view is held from the morally sophisticated position of commitment is that someone holding the view can honestly and completely present the opposite view in a factual, nondisparaging way. It is not easy for a student to hear that her opinion might actually reflect the polarized stage of duality rather than commitment to well-reasoned judgment.

For example, one semester a pro-choice activist in my Ethics and Public Affairs class decided to do her paper on women's ability to obtain abortions in states where it was increasingly difficult to find doctors willing to perform late-term or even midterm abortions. Another student, a pro-life sympathizer, felt strongly that protests and activities to shut down clinics that performed abortions were justified in protecting the lives of unborn babies. Both students had difficulty with the research and dispassionate writing necessary to complete part II of their papers. The pro-choice student certainly did not want to have a discussion with the director of Birthright, as I required. The pro-life student was not happy that I required her to talk with the director of our local Planned Parenthood. But the result of insisting that the students seriously listen to and present views in opposition with their own gave them the challenge of clarifying their positions and stipulating the limitations of their own views. When they wrote the analysis sections of their papers, they turned out to be surprisingly similar in describing under what conditions abortions were morally permitted and when they were not.

Part III of the semester-long paper asks students to make normative judgments. Students are asked, "Drawing on what you have laid out in part I and part II, what in this case is morally permitted? What is morally prohibited?

What is morally ideal?" The students draw conclusions where they can. They are also asked to clarify the areas about which they are still uncertain. Encouraging students to make tentative conclusions keeps them from retreating to the safety of polarization. Feeling uncertain and confused about some aspects of a case is intellectually honest. Professional scholars acknowledge the limitations of their conclusions. Students should be encouraged to do the same.

When we identify a range of morally permitted behaviors rather than seek to state one right action, we imply that some behaviors can be morally permitted without all of them being what we might individually choose to do. This is a tolerance of difference that transcends the unwillingness to make normative judgments. The ability to argue to a range of morally permitted behavior illustrates commitment with uncertainty rather than fatalistic relativism.

A RETURN TO FATALISTIC RELATIVISM

Whether we examine Kohlberg's, Gilligan's, or Perry's scheme of moral development, relativism is the mark of a transition from one stage to the next. From Kohlberg's perspective, a person who is just beginning to seek the approval of others may well be overwhelmed by the differences between who approves of which action. Later on, as a person gives up reliance on rules as a basis for deciding what is right, it is natural for him or her to experience a degree of ambivalence. If rules don't provide the answers, how is one to figure out a better way?

From Gilligan's point of view, the transition between care for others and care for all can result in a feeling of hopelessness that the goal is simply impossible. If you can't meet everyone's needs, who's to say whose needs take priority?

Perry clearly defines relativism as a step between dualism and commitment with uncertainty.

People who are feeling relativistic need to know that it is safe to not know, right now, how they should judge a particular situation. But they can also be challenged to explore the boundaries of their relativism. Rather than argue for the best choice, it might be easier to talk about what would be absolutely wrong for someone to do and why. Perhaps we can describe a range of acceptable behaviors if we were the person in question.

Teaching ethics in a way that promotes students' and teachers' moral growth and development is a daunting task. It is tempting for teachers to provoke students to shake them out of their complacency or avoidance of moral responsibility. It is tempting to ignore behavior that threatens or disrupts carefully crafted lesson plans. But both approaches suggest that the teacher is reasoning in a dogmatic rather than sophisticated way about his or her own beliefs. More important, these acts do not reflect Gilligan's requirement of nonviolence that she argues is necessary for the ethical outcome of any dilemma—even the dilemma of how to best teach ethics.

NOTES

1. Daniel Callahan, "Goals in the Teaching of Ethics," in *Ethics Teaching in Higher Education*, ed. Daniel Callahan and Sissela Bok (New York: Plenum, 1980), 69–70.

2. Hastings Center, "Summary Recommendations," in *Ethics Teaching in Higher Education*, ed. Daniel Callahan and Sissela Bok (New York: Plenum, 1980), 300.

3. Clifford Christians and Michael Traber, eds., *Communication Ethics and Universal Values* (Thousand Oaks, CA: Sage, 1997), 341.

4. James Q. Wilson, *The Moral Sense* (New York: Free Press, 1993), 12.

5. Lawrence Kohlberg, *The Psychology of Moral Development: The Nature and Validity of Stages* (San Francisco: Harper & Row, 1984), 35–62.

6. See, for example, Seyla Benhabib, *Critique, Norm and Utopia: A Study of the Foundations of Critical Theory* (New York: Columbia University Press, 1986); H. Cantril, *The Pattern of Human Concerns* (New Brunswick, NJ: Rutgers University Press, 1965); James Q. Wilson, *The Moral Sense* (New York: Free Press, 1993).

7. Kohlberg's highest stage is controversial in that, toward the end of his life, he postulated a seventh stage that is based on a combination of spiritual and ethical orientation. However, the majority of his work postulates stage 6 as a final stage of moral sophistication.

8. The most complete descriptions of Kohlberg's work can be found in the following two volumes: *Essays on Moral Development, I: The Philosophy of Moral Development* (San Francisco: Harper & Row, 1981) and *Essays on Moral Development, II: The Psychology of Moral Development* (San Francisco: Harper & Row, 1984).

9. Jean Piaget, *The Origins of Intelligence in Children* (New York: International Universities Press, 1952).

10. Carol Gilligan, *In a Different Voice: Psychological Theory and Women's Development* (Cambridge: Harvard University Press, 1982).

11. Carol Gilligan, "New Maps of Development: New Visions of Maturity," *American Journal of Orthopsychiatry* 52, no. 2 (1982): 210.

12. Carol Gilligan, "In a Different Voice: Women's Conception of Self and Morality," in *Stage Theories of Cognitive and Moral Development: Criticisms and Applications*, ed. Harvard Educational Review (Cambridge: Harvard Educational Review, 1978), 52–89.

13. Gilligan, *Different Voice: Psychological Theory*, 174.

14. William Perry, *Forms of Intellectual and Ethical Development in the College Years* (New York: Holt, Rinehart and Winston, 1970).

15. Students are also introduced to research ethics in that they are required to prepare protocols for submission to the university's Institutional Review Board. While most of the projects will be judged "exempt" from review, it is important that students realize that even their fledgling research can make people vulnerable.

Chapter Six

Integrated Case Analysis

Case studies are the staples of ethics discussions. But the discussants may have wildly different understandings of a case. Each reader brings his or her own perceptions and projections to the analysis.

That is what I learned some years ago while developing a course in research ethics for graduate students of science and medicine. My faculty colleagues at Dartmouth and I decided that pretest analysis of a case at the beginning of the term and a second analysis of the same case at the end would demonstrate what students learned during the course. The case we chose, *Misconduct: Caltech's Trial by Fire*, told the story of Vipin Kumar, a postdoctoral candidate, and James Urban, a graduate student, who worked in a laboratory at California Technological University run by distinguished scientist Leroy Hood.[1] That laboratory included more than sixty-five junior investigators, lab assistants, and students.

In late 1990, it looked as though Kumar and Urban had acted in ways that were not acceptable in the practice of science. Kumar falsified a lab result. A figure that was supposed to show DNA from several cell lines had the same pattern among the lines. From carefully looking at the artifacts—the little spots that crop up on gels—it was clear that Kumar had used data from just a few cell lines, duplicated them, and then labeled them as though they came from many more cell lines. Kumar did not deny doctoring the figure. He said he did not know that this kind of duplication was unacceptable practice. When these facts were disclosed, Hood withdrew a paper that had been accepted for publication.

On top of that, some of Kumar's raw data turned out to be missing. Kumar maintained that two of his lab notebooks that confirmed questionable data had been stolen.

While reviewing Kumar's work, two committees—one internal to the lab and the other a university investigatory committee—discovered irregularities in the work of a graduate student, James Urban. Urban had served as coauthor on some of Kumar's papers. As in Kumar's case, much of Urban's data was mysteriously missing. Urban claimed he threw it away when he moved to take a job at the University of Chicago. The committees concluded that a final paper, published in the October 20, 1989, issue of *Cell*, contained data different from the paper that Urban had sent for review and that the data in the first draft were fabricated. Urban did not deny the charge, but he did deny intent to deceive. One official close to the case said that Urban intended to do the work and assumed that he knew how it would turn out.

Urban was already working at another university by the time the investigation uncovered the irregularities, but Kumar was still working in the Hood lab. Kumar had applied for several jobs, with Hood's strong recommendation. Before the investigation was complete, Hood told the following that Kumar was under investigation: universities to which Kumar had applied for jobs, journals that had accepted or published papers based on Kumar's results, and the funding agencies (National Institutes of Health and National Science Foundation) that had provided the needed resources for Kumar's work. Washington University, which had offered Kumar a job, withdrew the offer.

When our students at Dartmouth examined this case for their pretest, faculty expected students to understand that Kumar and Urban had done wrong. We hoped that, at the end of the course, they would recognize more subtle issues, such as what the lab director and university should do and not do when investigating a case of alleged research misconduct.

We asked three independent external reviewers to conduct a structured content analysis on the students' pre- and posttests. We were perplexed when our reviewers disagreed on what the students understood. For example, the three evaluators did not agree on whom a particular student had identified as moral agents. We had asked evaluators to count as a "moral agent" any person whom the student recognized as being accountable for some action. When we first reviewed the evaluations, before our own reading of the student essays, it had not occurred to us that the problem could be with the students rather than with the evaluators.

Kumar and Urban, whom faculty had identified as the "impossible to miss" moral agents, were instead identified as victims by many of the graduate students. Some students said that no one taught Urban how to write an article or his thesis. Some said that no one taught Kumar how to record cell lines. The lab director and senior faculty in the lab, according to our students, were too busy with their own careers and research agendas to provide sufficient mentoring. This perspective remained consistent between pre- and posttests, although the students responded as we expected in class discussions with faculty facilitation.

It was suddenly clear to us that our students were analyzing the Kumar/ Urban case based on their own experiences. They identified with the graduate student and the postdoc and were expressing their anger at what they perceived as their own mentors' neglect of them.

Through this experience, I realized that good cases provoke projection from readers as surely as they test a reader's ability to analyze the facts of a case. When presented with a case, we readers need to realize that we bring our own assumptions to it. An advantage of group discussion is that personal assumptions are called into question. Individual perspectives might change as a result of hearing how others have understood a case or a situation.

This chapter describes a method for analyzing cases. It also addresses the need to think about making moral mistakes. While the vast majority of cases focuses on wrongdoing, practical ethics literature is overwhelmingly silent on the fact that most of us, at least occasionally, knowingly choose to do wrong. Some literature addresses the forgiveness of others but is silent on the forgiveness of self or how easy it is to rationalize wrongdoing.

Few among us always choose to do what we think is the morally ideal act. Sometimes we don't even choose to do what is morally permitted or required. From time to time, we do things that we know are wrong. Whether the transgression is a lie to avoid feared consequences or even an unwanted social engagement or is an impulsive choice to be rude to a colleague or a stranger on the street, we have done things that we believed to be wrong at the time, or soon after.

Awareness that one has knowingly done wrong is an important step in moral growth. Sometimes people have to make the wrong choice before understanding, morally and psychologically, what makes the action wrong. There may be some unjustifiable acts that we continue to choose throughout a lifetime without recognizing the moral weight of our actions.

Reading and discussing cases should encourage readers to reflect on how they act in analogous situations in their own lives. It is easy to argue that some hypothetical character in a case study should do his or her duty regardless of cost to self. It is more difficult to recognize the times that I have chosen not to meet a responsibility and to consider what I should do. The former is an intellectual exercise. The latter is doing ethics in the first person.

ESSENTIALS OF A GOOD CASE

A well-prepared case will allow for reader identification with one or more decision makers. Unfortunately, in the pretest and posttest for the Dartmouth research ethics class, the only decision makers who provided natural identification for the students reading the case were the graduate student and post-doc charged with wrongdoing. Upon reflection, it is not surprising that our own graduate students would recast Kumar and Urban in a way that made our students more comfortable with that identification. They perceived Kumar and Urban, like them, as powerless underlings caught up in a system not of their making. And consider what follows from a perception that one is powerless: As was discussed in the previous chapter on moral development, individuals who perceive themselves as powerless do not see themselves as morally accountable for their actions. They excuse themselves by believing they cannot be blamed for what they are doing because they are victims of the system.

As with the case described at the beginning of this chapter, cases can be short and relatively simple, with the intent of focusing reader attention on the recognition of moral agents (Kumar, Urban, Caltech, lab director, investigatory committees, other universities, journal editors, funding agencies) and on the limits of acceptable choices by each of these. Cases can also be several pages of narrative or hours of audio or video, giving participants the opportunity to find the ethical aspects of a case in a virtual haystack of other issues and considerations. Practice with both kinds of cases is needed to develop conscious skill in analysis.

SYSTEMATIC MORAL ANALYSIS

Systematic moral analysis (SMA) is the process of dissecting a case or a potential choice of action in a step-by-step way to ensure that no ethical aspect is ignored.[2] A good analysis is *systematic* in two ways. First, it provides a general system, or process, to be followed in any case analysis. It is also systematic in that it is based on theoretical foundation that provides conceptual support for each step taken in the analysis. A system is based on theory.

The example of systematic moral analysis presented in this chapter is based, in large part, upon the theory of contemporary moral philosopher Bernard Gert. Gert uses a combination of concepts and questions from the classics to develop his own theory. His process of analysis is thus a good contemporary example of mixed formalism. However, what follows in this chapter does not adhere strictly to Gert. I have added to Gert's process my own understandings from classical moral philosophy along with questions and considerations derived from contemporary feminist analysis. The five questions derived from classical and feminist philosophy, included in chapter 4, are implicit in the more specific steps of analysis included in this chapter.[3]

A PROCESS OF SYSTEMATIC MORAL ANALYSIS

Any person who has the power to intentionally affect members of the moral community or subjects of moral worth is a moral agent. Agency requires knowledge of general facts about the world, namely that "persons can be killed by other persons and they do not normally want to be killed; one person can inflict pain or disable another person and persons do not normally want to be inflicted with pain or disabled; one person can deprive another person of freedom or pleasure and persons do not normally want to be deprived of these things."[4]

Because moral agents realize these general facts, agents have the obligation to refrain from causing harms such as death, pain, disability, or deprivation of freedom or pleasure unless there is adequate justification for doing so. The obligation to refrain from causing harm applies impartially to everyone whom an agent may encounter.

Case analysis includes two distinct levels. The first level, which is necessary, and sometimes sufficient, I call *conceptualization*; the second level, which is not always necessary and never sufficient alone, I call *justification*. Conceptualization is the step in which one clarifies the ethical issues, identifies agents, and determines who could be reasonably held blameworthy or praiseworthy within the situation. The level of justification is when one figures out if there is adequate reason for causing harm. At this level, one explains why some acts are morally prohibited, others are morally permitted, some are required, and yet others are morally ideal.

Step One: Conceptualization

Conceptualization is the necessary first step of ethical analysis. Many analyses can be concluded at this level. This level identifies particular acts as morally questionable. Once an act is properly identified as an act of cheating or deception, for example, it may be obvious that the act cannot be justified. Many people who are willing to defend an act—if they rationalize that their choice falls short of "real" deception—recognize the difficulty in justifying the act once it can be shown that what they propose is, indeed, real deception.

On the other hand, if an action can be shown not to be an example of deception in the conceptualization stage of analysis (e.g., the reporter had no duty to tell the story source being interviewed about other information that had been revealed), there is no need to justify the action. Only actions that can be shown to be morally questionable require further analysis.

The first step is to determine if harm has been (or is likely to be) caused. Gert's analysis begins with an understanding that there are harms we all want to avoid: death, pain, disability, being deprived of freedom or pleasure.[5] If someone causes himself or herself to suffer one of these harms without reason, that action would qualify as irrational; if someone does it to another without adequate reason, that action is unethical. Gert identifies ten moral rules that coincide with the harms that can be caused by self and others.

1. Don't kill.
2. Don't cause pain.[6]
3. Don't disable.
4. Don't deprive of freedom.[7]
5. Don't deprive of pleasure.
6. Don't deceive.
7. Keep your promise.
8. Don't cheat.[8]
9. Obey the law.
10. Do your duty.[9]

The first step in conceptualization, then, answers the three following questions:

1. Is a member of the moral community or subject of moral worth being caused harm?
2. Has a moral agent caused the harm?
3. What are the agent's role-related responsibilities?

The next step in conceptualization is to establish whether a moral agent is potentially blameworthy or not, leading to the next question to be answered:

4. Was harm intended or could it have been predicted?

The Nature of Role-Related Responsibilities

As a professor, I have responsibilities to my students and to the department and university that employ me. I have responsibilities toward other ethics scholars. Defining an agent's role-related responsibilities as they relate to the situation at hand is necessary before one can decide if there has been a neglect of duties (violation of moral rule ten).

We all have multiple roles. I am a wife, a daughter, a sister, and a friend in my personal life. I am a teacher, a scholar, a news source, a colleague in my professional life. Each of these roles, and the many that don't come to mind at the moment, carries a unique set of obligations.

It can be difficult to be specific about role-related responsibilities. I suggest thinking of oneself as an alien anthropologist, sent to find people doing a good job of representing the role that one is seeking to describe. What would the journalist be doing? How is the journalist different from other mass communication professionals? A good description of role-related responsibilities should be twenty-five words or less and should show how the role in question is different from other similar roles in society. It is better to clarify role-related responsibilities before doing detailed analysis of a case so that the description of role is not tailored to provide a specific answer for the case at hand.

Identification of role-related responsibilities provides a basis for determining if moral rule ten, do your duty, has been violated. Role-related responsibilities will also be useful in step two, justification of the SMA, for determining if there have been adequate reasons for the agent to violate moral rules.

Blameworthiness and Praiseworthiness

Sometimes people are hurt without some person being blameworthy for that harm. A situation is morally questionable if it is found that the harm was caused by violation of one or more moral rules. However, an agent can be a proximate cause of an event without being morally blameworthy for the harm that follows that event.

For example, if I were to stop my car at a pedestrian crosswalk to allow someone to cross, I am not blameworthy for the damage caused to the driver behind me who stopped only when he crashed into the back end of my car. Indeed, if the force of that crash was so overwhelming that it propelled my vehicle forward and I ended up running over the person I had stopped to avoid, I would still not be blameworthy. There is a difference between being the proximate cause for an event and being morally blameworthy for its outcome.

However, if I recognized the person in the crosswalk as someone I wished to harm and also recognized that the driver of the car behind me was not paying attention, and *then* I slammed on my brakes with the hope that the driver of the car behind me would crash into my car, propelling it forward into the person I despised, I would indeed be morally blameworthy for any injury caused. I would be morally blameworthy in this case, even if my actions were legally judged as unintended. The difference, in this case, is my intent.

An agent has acted in a morally questionable way (is potentially morally blameworthy) if any of these conditions apply:

- The harm to the person (P) came about because the agent (A) neglected to fulfill his or her role-related responsibilities.
- A acted with intention to cause harm to P.
- A could have reasonably predicted the harm caused as a consequence of A's action or nonaction and could have accomplished the same legitimate end while causing no harm or less harm.

An alternative way to think about blameworthiness is that any person who has the power to affect a situation should be held blameworthy for choosing not to use that power to avoid or limit harm. Therefore, an alternative and less minimalist way of judging blameworthiness is this: If A could be held morally praiseworthy for a good outcome in an event, he or she should be held morally blameworthy for a bad outcome in the event.

Once it is clear that one or more moral rules have been (or are likely to be) violated, and that one or more moral agents could be held morally blameworthy for the action, the conceptualization phase of the systematic moral analysis is complete.

If no moral rules have been violated by an agent, he or she cannot be held morally blameworthy for the act. However, it does not follow that the person should be praised for it, either. Praiseworthy actions are generally those that prevent or mitigate harm, not those that simply do not cause harm.

Step Two: Justification

The steps in the analysis of justification consider whether the morally questionable action could be morally permitted in the particular situation and in all that are similar. Justification starts with the analysis of identified moral rule violations:

1. Which harms are caused by the violation of the rule? Which harms are avoided? Which harms are prevented?[10] Gert reminds us that foreseen and foreseeable consequences are important criteria for consideration, along with actual or intended consequences. Agents cannot ethically ignore the unintended, but predictable, consequences of their actions.

It is also important to notice that every unjustified violation of a moral rule invariably causes some harm. The direct harms are obvious—someone is killed, caused pain or disability, or is deprived of freedom or pleasure. The indirect harms are less obvious. But deception, promise breaking, cheating, disobeying the law, and neglecting one's duty create predictable harms for individuals, for the community as a whole, and for agents themselves. With an act of deception, for example, the person deceived is caused harm by being led to a false conclusion even if this person does not know he was deceived. The person will make choices or judgments based on the faulty claim. Community is harmed by each act of deception because societal relationships are based on trust and truth. Deceptive acts break down societal trust even if the deceiver is the only one who ever knows. The agent knows herself to be the kind of person who will deceive in these circumstances. As it is natural for us to analogize that others are like ourselves, the act of lying decreases societal trust because the liar suspects that others are liars too. We have learned from Aristotle and our own experience that liars and truth tellers are created by practice and known by their habits.

2. What are the relevant desires and beliefs of the person toward whom the rule is being violated?[11] Refraining from providing clinical treatment to a terminal patient, which would generally be morally prohibited, becomes morally permitted (perhaps, even morally ideal) when the caregiver has the dying person's consent. Some people who are dying want to know details of their condition, even if such knowledge causes them pain. It is not justified to withhold this information from these patients. However, other terminally ill patients prefer not to know clinical details. It is justified to withhold information from them with their consent.

3. "Is the relationship between the agent and the person toward whom the rule is being violated such that the former has a duty to violate moral rules with regard to the latter independent of their consent?"[12] The presence of a special relationship can make the difference in whether consent is morally required. The relationship between parents and their minor children and between governments and their citizens can allow for the former to deprive the latter of pleasure or freedom without consent. Parents have the special role-related responsibility to raise their children. Therefore, they have the unique right to control them. Government has the special duty of protecting citizens, so it has the unique privilege of taking money from them in the form of taxes so that it can perform its duties. In contrast, while professors sometimes cause their students pain with honest evaluations or deprive students of pleasure by giving them assignments, their doing so is with the students' consent. Being a student is a voluntary act.

4. "Which goods (including kind, degree, probability, duration, and distribution) are promoted by the violation?"[13] The goods being promoted provide added justification in cases that are already justified by consent or special relationship, or in cases of justified paternalism.

5. Is the rule being violated toward people in order to prevent them from violating moral rules when the violation would be (1) unjustified or (2) weakly justified?[14] For example, it is morally justified to detain a person on false pretenses when that person is threatening to murder another.

6. Is the rule being violated toward people because they have violated moral rules (1) unjustifiably or (2) with weak justification?[15] The answer to this question justifies punishment, whether in the form of a judge's sending someone to prison or a professor's giving a student an F for plagiarism. It is important to remember that, in these examples, the judge and professor are causing harm. However, causing harm in these cases is justified.

7. Are there any alternative actions or policies that would not violate moral rules?[16] The primary responsibility for all moral agents is to find ways to meet their role-related responsibilities in a way that causes the least amount of harm, even when causing some harm can be justified. This is also the time to make sure that actions are chosen that take into account the needs of those involved as well as their right not to have moral rules violated toward them. It is also time to step back to look at the big picture. Cases for analysis happen in a larger context of ongoing relationships and the network of relationships we call community. Ethically ideal choices reflect all these considerations.

A final consideration is whether the agent could publicly allow the violation. For example, some acts of deception are justified by the ability to make that act known to all relevant parties. Unmarked police cars are an example of justified acts of deception. The police in these cases are disguising themselves as nonpolice. Generally, citizens correctly expect officers of the law to identify themselves as such. It is an example of cheating when police fail to meet this expectation. However, citizens have agreed, at least implicitly, that having unmarked police cars might be useful in preventing people from speeding and in protecting the public.

Analysis of the case using the questions in step two should, minimally, yield a description and explanation of which actions are morally required (by the agent's role-related responsibilities) and which are morally prohibited (unjustified violations of moral rules). The goal is to have the analysis, in addition, yield a list of actions which are morally permitted (actions that don't violate moral rules or violations that are justified) and morally ideal (actions that prevent harms and promote the good without causing harms).

AN EXAMPLE OF SYSTEMATIC
MORAL ANALYSIS

In the late 1980s, coproducers Wendy Conquest, Bob Drake, and I wrote and produced a twenty-seven-minute video documentary, *Buying Time: The Media Role in Health Care.*[17] The case presented the story of two patients in need of bone marrow transplants: Sue Jackman, a thirty-three-year-old Vermont resident whose insurer initially refused to cover the transplant, and Derek Annesse, a six-year-old New Hampshire Medicaid recipient. The state had declined to cover his transplant. Both cases came to the attention of local news media, who publicized the cases. Ultimately, Blue Cross/Blue Shield of Vermont agreed to pay for Jackman's transplant, and New Hampshire Medicaid agreed to pay for Annesse's transplant.

Our documentary presented the story of how news media got involved in the reporting of those cases and how the news coverage ultimately changed policy. Because of the news coverage of Sue Jackman, Vermont Blue Cross/Blue Shield became the first Blue Cross/Blue Shield in the United States to cover bone marrow transplants for the treatment of breast cancer. Because of the news coverage of Derek Annesse, New Hampshire Medicaid changed its policy to cover bone marrow transplants for patients under the age of twenty-one. Relevant ethical issues were raised through an examination of the perceptions of state representatives, media professionals, and policy analysts as well as those of the bone marrow recipients and their families and friends. The documentary was an example of a descriptive case presentation, with no normative judgments offered by the filmmakers.

Buying Time was meant to show a real-life dilemma with real patients, families, and professionals struggling hard to cope with tough ethical choices. The best presentations are those made by investigators who have not figured out the "right" answer. I did not attempt to do a systematic case analysis of the issues in *Buying Time* until the documentary had been completed and released. I suspended my judgment, just as I ask students to do when they are researching and writing an ethics case for analysis. The job of the case writer is, first, to be a good journalist, honestly presenting as many perspectives as possible.

What follows is the systematic moral analysis I ultimately conducted of the issues in *Buying Time*. Notes relating to the steps of my systematic moral analysis appear in [brackets].

Compassion and Responsiveness in Professional Ethics

[First, I start with my conclusion.] *Buying Time* provides a good example of journalists doing the wrong thing for the right reasons and of policy makers doing the right thing for the wrong reasons. It was wrong for journalists to champion the cases of Sue and Derek, but they intervened for what seemed to be a good reason: compassion. It was right for policy makers to provide bone marrow transplants for breast cancer and myelodysplasia, but they did so for a problematic reason: media pressure.

[Next, I begin with the first level of analysis, conceptualization.] It is difficult to get a handle on the ethical problem for journalists in *Buying Time* because it looks like a simple problem of fairness, but it isn't. It is easy to say, "News organizations should be fair. If the mother of another six-year-old child calls these reporters a week later with the same story, well, the newspaper should do a story on that child too." Unfortunately, even if news organizations were willing to publicize and thus help fund-raise for every patient's plight, it wouldn't work. News media cannot take every case of need to the public and get the same public response. Citizens are not going to respond to pleas for help week after week. Providing the same coverage for everyone in the same situation would not be effective. Nor would it be news.

It is difficult to get to the bottom of the policy makers' problem because it seems that the policy makers did the right thing. They responded to public outcry. If we have a representative government (or an insurance company that is responsive to the desires of those it insures), we would think that policy makers should do what the people want. But the problem is in deciding *which* people ought to be represented. To *which* public outcry should officials respond? The rule that policy makers in *Buying Time* seemed to follow was this: you'll get what you need if you can get media attention or if you are lucky enough to have the same kind of problem as the people who got media attention.

Because of Derek Annesse, New Hampshire Medicaid now provides a bone marrow transplant for all people in need of it who are under twenty-one years of age. It sounds as if the state officials are acting fairly because they created a policy to benefit all others like Derek. This sounds less fair, however, when we realize that the money now going to fund these bone marrow transplants is coming out of the same pot that funds prenatal care and standard medical care for other indigent children. Some needy people are being deprived to help other needy people. At the time that Derek's case came to the state's attention, legal services lawyers in the state had been working to negotiate an increase in how much the state paid for prenatal services. No doctors in Derek's hometown were taking in new pregnant Medicaid patients because, at the time, Medicaid was paying less than one third of what practitioners charged for prenatal visits. Just when the state was ready to approve a rate hike for prenatal doctor visits, the Derek Annesse case came to the attention of the governor. In response to the governor's decision to fund

Annesse and patients like him, the state legislature decided they'd better hold on to that $400,000 in case they got more bone marrow cases.

That's not how government should function, even if the new policy was made in response to public pressure. In some puzzling way, we want a representative government that's somehow collectively smarter than the individual people it represents.

So, it doesn't help in analysis of the ethical issues in *Buying Time* if we classify the problem as a case of unfairness by the government or news media. Neither government nor news media can provide equally for everyone with extraordinary needs. Rather, it is important for journalists to stop acting out of compassion and for policy makers to stop being responsive to cases that get good press. Instead, both journalists and policy makers should do a more complete job of fulfilling their role-related responsibilities. [Now, I have clarified the issue we are dealing with in this case. It is not a case of fairness, which would lead one to an analysis of whether others were wrongly deprived of opportunity because of the professionals' actions. Rather, it is a case in which journalists and policy makers failed to do their duties. I will need to argue for why I make that claim before I can ponder whether the neglect of duty is morally justified or not.]

If journalists are doing their jobs, they provide readers and viewers with the information citizens need to make intelligent decisions for self-governance. It is morally permissible for journalists to do other things such as provide movie reviews and the crossword puzzle, but that's something they choose to do on top of what's morally required. Journalists are morally required to do the special duty associated with the job they have chosen.

If journalists were doing their jobs in telling us about bone marrow transplants, what would they report? What do citizens need to know about such things?

Citizens need to know about bone marrow transplants, that they work and how they work. And they need stories about how such discoveries are made. Citizens need to know how experimental or investigative procedures get funded. If insurance companies won't pay for this kind of clinical research, then who should? If it comes from the government, citizens need to hear stories about which kinds of research get chosen to be funded and which kinds do not.

Those were not the stories told by the journalists in *Buying Time*. Journalists did raise questions about the role of policy makers—in government and in insurance companies—but the questions they asked moved the public away from policy discussion.

Journalists asked, "How can you let this little boy die?" They didn't ask, "How are the decisions made about how to spread out that limited Medicaid budget?" They didn't ask, "Why is it so limited in the first place?" If they had asked those questions, the focus would have been on how the policy makers could best do their duty. [Here I detail the harms caused by journalists failing to do their duty. The harm is that citizens were not informed that policy makers failed to do their duty.

One duty of policy makers is to delineate a publicly known policy for how they distribute the public funds they control. The policy makers did not do that. Citizens were harmed by being deprived of the freedom (opportunity) to make educated decisions regarding their own self-governance, as they were not informed of governmental failure.]

Like journalists, policy makers have duties—role-related responsibilities—whether they are medical directors of insurance companies or state administrators of public health funds. One of the duties of government, as described by Gert,[18] is to prevent the suffering of harms (death, pain, disability) by its citizens. The state prevents suffering in a number of ways: enacts laws, establishes police departments, appoints judges to help enforce those laws, and builds jails. The state also supports medical research and the creation of medical property by funding research to help keep its citizens from suffering pain, disability, and death. The state taxes individuals to support the governmental duty.

It is an unanswered question of how aggressively the state ought to be working to prevent medical suffering by its citizens. Those who argue in favor of national health care conclude that the state has a moral obligation to provide health care as a way of preventing death, pain, and disability for its citizens. But regardless of the question of national health care, one can argue that policy makers have a duty to address the needs of deprived persons. A deprived person is someone who gets less than what we generally think every citizen should have.[19]

Whether a particular person should be included in the class of "deprived people" may be a matter of disagreement among rational people, but we can agree on some citizens that would surely be in that class. For example, homeless children living in poverty are examples of the class of deprived persons.

The duty-related question for policy makers in *Buying Time* is, then, twofold.

1. Are Derek and Sue deprived persons?
2. Are the policy makers shirking their duty toward other deprived persons in responding to Derek's and Sue's needs?

My answer to both questions is, "I don't know." The reason I don't know is that the state and the insurance company, respectively, neglected an important duty—that of developing defensible public criteria for how limited resources are to be distributed. The development of such criteria rightly belongs with the legislature—the people's representatives. In the case of *Buying Time*, the governmental decision was made not by the legislature but by the governor's office, in response to media pressure. Pressure was applied to the executive branch and it responded—by taking money that would have taken care of other needy people. This makes for neither a just nor a good government. By analogy, the same legislate-by-pressure rule applied to the insurance company. [Here I have established harms caused by policy makers' failure to do their duty. The harm caused is an unjustifiable policy that results in some people being harmed (caused pain, death, disability) when others in morally relevant similar situations are not. I also point out here what cannot be analyzed and why.]

Journalists, of course, had a corresponding duty to tell such stories.

And what if they did? If journalists tell these less dramatic policy stories, is it then okay for journalists to talk about individual people in need? I think not. [Here I move into the justification phase by examining alternative approaches and explaining why one approach is morally permitted and another is not.]

Social institutions, of which journalism, insurance companies, and government are instances, are different in a morally relevant way from individuals. Individuals should be compassionate; institutions ought not. There's a subtle irony that surfaces when news media act for the benefit of a single individual. In both Sue's and Derek's cases, we had journalists who were appalled at the lack of response from policy makers who could have helped these individuals in need. And they were right to be appalled. It's hard to justify a government or an agency denying treatment without compelling evidence that the denied treatment differs in kind from treatments allowed. But when journalists used the power of the press to bring about care for Sue and Derek, they became institutions that participated in the same uneven treatment they sought to expose. The assistance provided to a few does not make up for the harm caused to others by the intervention. [Here I described the harms caused, balanced against the harms avoided.]

The journalists' work implicitly asks, "How can these powerful institutions care for some and leave others in similar situations to die?" But when news media do the Sue story and the Derek story and ignore the Luther story and turn down the Nancy story, the news organization becomes just one more of those powerful institutions that care for some and leave others to die. We've already established that news organizations cannot treat every patient in similar situations in similar ways. Caring for individuals in the community is not the role-related responsibility of news organizations, as it is for governments or insurance companies. But the press is a powerful social institution, and it has a responsibility to use its power judiciously. When journalists identify an individual in need, with the clear implication that he or she will be directly assisted through news coverage, there should be a unique characteristic that can create a morally relevant difference from other similar cases of need. What makes the story "news" is not simply the identification of a particular person in need.

Like most ethical problems, *Buying Time* is an example of good people making the wrong decisions, often with the best of intentions. From the journalistic side, it's an example of what happens when good intentions get in the way of people doing their jobs. [My conclusion is that it was not morally justified for policy makers or journalists to neglect their duties in this case. Consider the SMA questions for justification:

Question 1: Which harms are caused by the violation of the rule? Which harms are avoided? Which harms are prevented? The harms caused include harm to the citizens from policy makers who are making policy without clear justification and from journalists who are failing to tell citizens the true news stories. Citizens are being deprived of the freedom (moral rule four) to make educated decisions regarding governmental policy. The harms being avoided are those to the two patients who are the subjects of these stories. The news stories as written are helping them avoid pain and death. But notice that both institutions (government and journalism) have primary responsibility to create policy that benefits the community as a whole. Neither institution would work effectively if it failed to meet institutional responsibilities in the hope of benefiting particular individuals.

Question 2: What are the relevant desires and beliefs of the person toward whom the rule is being violated? The primary rule being violated by journalists and policy makers is "Do your duty." Citizens (to whom journalists and policy makers have primary duty) would not want to be uninformed or to have unjust policies enacted.

Question 3: Does the agent have a duty to violate rules with regard to citizens? There is no special relationship to consider here between policy makers and Derek and Sue that does not exist between policy makers and all constituents. There is no special duty that would justify the deprivation of citizens' knowledge and choice.

Question 4: Which goods are promoted by the violation? Potentially lifesaving treatment for Sue and Derek and those clinically similar, but the lack of lifesaving treatment for those deprived by the policy to fund Sue and Derek and clinically similar cases. While it is always sad when an individual does not get life-sustaining medical care—and ideally, we would live in a world where that would not happen—the community as a whole is best served by social institutions with policies that allow for equal access to public goods.

Questions 5 and 6 are not relevant to this case, as the social institutions are not acting in response to other moral rule violations.

Question 7: Are there alternatives that do not violate moral rules, that recognize needs, and that focus on the picture bigger than the individuals in this case? There are, indeed, preferable alternatives to the journalistic action taken in publicizing these two cases. Stories could have been written that addressed the larger issues and focused policy makers' and citizens' attention on creating just policies. Policy makers could have enacted policies based on an analysis of aggregate public good rather than on media pressure and could have engaged citizens in deciding what types of medical care will be paid through public or insured funds and which will not. Individuals are not being treated unethically if some who participate in a publicly known process, such as lining up to get tickets to a performance, are denied service (e.g., because there is no more seating). Similarly, individuals who are denied funds for certain treatment because the community has determined that it is better overall for limited funds to be committed for some purpose but not another are not being treated unethically. But if the process is not determined in a justified way, it is not justified for individuals to be denied.

LIFE AFTER THE MORAL MISTAKE

Buying Time provides a good example of how one would expect most case analyses to turn out: There was no inherent evil in the case, but there were professional mistakes. These mistakes were ethical in nature because the policy makers and journalists failed to meet their role-related responsibilities. They failed to do their duties. When one fails to do one's duty, even out of ignorance rather than intention, that person has made a moral mistake. If we had been the principals in *Buying Time*, now recognizing that we made mistakes, though we were well intentioned, what follows? An agent in such situations should consider the following:

1. Could I have made different decisions? If the agent is unwilling or unable to realize that she could have made different choices, she cannot recognize that she has made a moral mistake. Denial of alternative possibilities precludes moral growth.
2. If I had been a journalist or working in the insurance company or governmental agency, how could I have encouraged my organization to make better choices? The agent should recognize his power to bring

about change in the institution, if the problem is at an institutional level. Perception of oneself as a victim of circumstance, unable to affect change, also precludes moral growth.

3. How can I formulate a plan of action to make a difference the next time this issue comes up? Recognizing a moral problem doesn't do much good if the agent finds herself or the organization simply repeating the violation.

THE IMPORTANCE OF RECOGNIZING
MORAL MISTAKES

I have argued throughout this book that the primary reason for ethics education is for those engaged in the study, teacher and student alike, to be motivated to become increasingly better decision makers about ethical issues. Therefore, it is vital to recognize moral mistakes when they happen. Far too often, we rationalize or excuse our mistakes rather than accept them as signs of ethical failure and opportunities for further growth.

What follows is a list of excuses commonly used to avoid recognizing that one has made a moral mistake:

1. *Other people do it.* Recently, I explained to students in my professional ethics class why I required them to get Institutional Review Board (IRB) clearance for projects involving interviews or surveys. The students, understandably, wanted to get on with their research. Their argument for why they should not have to seek IRB approval was that other professors had not required them to do so. Their attempt to justify unethical behavior by pointing to the unethical behavior of others led to a fruitful discussion. The students weren't necessarily convinced that I had good reason for requiring them to get IRB approval, but they were able to see that using the argument that other people get away with it did not provide a basis upon which to advance their argument.

2. *My boss told me to do it.* This rationalization is a variation on the excuse that other people do the unethical act. The reasoning here is that if one is following the direction of a superior, the person committing the act is not responsible for the consequences. However, as long as the agent is not the subject of coercion or threat, moral responsibility is not transferable from actor to authority. It is easy for people to accept that they are independent autonomous agents until they would prefer not to accept the responsibility of their actions. Then the heteronomous influ-

ence of others, particularly of authority figures, provides an easy-to-use excuse. But it is yet one more form of denial.

3. *Moral rules are nice in theory but don't work in practice.* Philosopher John Dewey might have made this point best in his observation that people wave the banner of principle but march to the drummer of expediency. While we can easily come up with examples that prove this to be true, it doesn't follow that the principles or rules should be ignored. We should not expect humans to consistently behave in accordance with what is morally required, permitted, or ideal, but we should expect them to recognize rather than excuse those mistakes. We should expect ourselves and others to strive to do the best that we can.

4. *I didn't mean to hurt anybody.* Often people commit harms unintentionally. But when harm could be predicted or when harm is the result of an agent's neglecting his or her role-related responsibility, the agent is responsible for harm caused, even if that person had the best of intentions. The lack of intentionality works to mitigate the level of one's responsibility, but it does not deny responsibility.

5. *No one knew.* If ethics is a first-person activity, then the intentions, motivations, and outcomes are, indeed, known to the person who matters most—the agent. The lack of external consequences for an act is not the basis upon which one should judge the moral permissibility of his or her behavior.

NOTES

1. Edited and abstracted from L. Roberts, "Misconduct: Trial by Fire," *Science* 243 (1991): 1344–1347.

2. This chapter does not provide the theoretical backing for the steps included in the SMA. There is not time nor space here, or in a semester-long practical ethics class, to argue for this process over others. However, as few people have a conscious process, this SMA provides tools that individuals can use and that allow group discussion about a case to take place. Many group discussions about ethics fail because participants are not using terms in the same way or because they do not agree on what is ethically relevant. Once my students are able to use this SMA effectively, they are free to challenge it or argue for alternative methods of consideration.

3. The impartiality required by Kant is necessary to conduct the SMA included in this chapter. Every person deserves the same basic moral protections (don't violate moral rules in regard to me without adequate justification). These considerations are specifically addressed in questions 1–3 of the conceptualization stage. The steps regarding justification in this chapter (and specifically questions 3–5) address goods and should be considered in Mill's aggregate sense. Question 7 is Aristotelian in that it asks us to go beyond what is morally permitted and to seek an action that might be morally ideal—to act as our moral

hero might. This question also asks us to consider the needs of those involved, relation-ships, and community. Thinking of a case from a basis of needs and with consideration of the bigger picture can reveal alternatives that are not visible from close analysis of the specific case alone.

4. Bernard Gert, *Morality: Its Nature and Justification* (New York: Oxford University Press, 2005), 24.

5. This list, and all application of Gert that follows, has been edited, interpreted, and enhanced. Its inclusion does not imply Gert's approval of my changes and additions.

6. This includes emotional pain.

7. Freedom is meant to include opportunity to act. Failure to disclose information can deprive people of opportunity to act knowledgeably.

8. Cheating means that one fails to meet others' reasonable expectations of him or her.

9. Gert, *Morality*, 159–219.

10. Gert, *Morality*, 227.

11. Gert, *Morality*, 228.

12. Gert, *Morality*, 230.

13. Gert, *Morality*, 230.

14. Gert, *Morality*, 231.

15. Gert, *Morality*, 232.

16. Gert, *Morality*, 232.

17. As an illustration that there is no obvious conflict between self-interest and ethics, the video documentary *Buying Time* is available for purchase or rent from Fanlight Pro-ductions, ISBN 1-57295-133-8.

18. Gert, *Morality*, 364–371.

19. Gert, *Morality*, 371–372.

Chapter Seven

A Bridge across Cultures

Henrietta Mann, then professor of social work at the University of Montana, faced thirty-one undergraduate students enrolled in her Native American Religion and Philosophy class one day in the 2000 spring semester. She had invited me in to observe an approach to teaching practical ethics that was different from that used by those of us trained in Western philosophy. Professor Mann was dressed in a clay-colored shirt, hand painted with Native American symbols. Her hair, short-cropped on the sides, sported a waist-length braid in the back. At 66, she was an elder in her tribe, the Southern Cheyenne.

"I am finally a woman of wisdom," she told the class with pride. "You don't get there until you are 65."

"Sweet Medicine and Erect Horns," she said, as she wrote the names on the board. "These are our prophets. They brought us our ceremonies and our teaching. They show us how the values of the people are reflected in our ceremonies. They gave us the ceremonies to remind us of the four substances used to create the world."

This class didn't look or feel like the ethics courses I had taken or taught, yet it was one of the forty-two free-standing courses at the University of Montana approved to provide students with upper-level general-education credits in ethics and human values. At the University of Montana, the general-education criteria were purposefully written broadly enough to encompass ways of examining ethics that transcended the content and processes of dominant society. The students in the class, many of whom appeared to be Anglo, listened intently to Professor Mann's descriptions and explanations.

"The first day of the Sun Dance, we make the rattles," she said.

"The Cheyenne traditionally know that it is time to prepare for Sun Dance when the leaves of the cottonwood tree curl up toward the sun. Now, to accommodate the workday requirements imposed by the dominant culture, the five-day celebration begins on the Wednesday before the weekend closest to the summer solstice. It is easier to negotiate vacation time based on set dates for the ceremony rather than by explaining to a white boss that the cottonwood trees say it is time."

The Native students in the class nodded their heads appreciatively and with new understanding. The myths, adages, rules, and trinkets that were woven into their daily routines on the reservation now begin to make rational sense as well. As Mann helped Anglo students understand what was, to them, a foreign culture and approach to understanding the responsibilities of human beings, she was also providing some of the Native students with new ways of appreciating their own cultures. From childhood, these students had learned to be silent rather than show disrespect by questioning their elders' ways. For some of them, this was the first explanation of their traditions that they had heard that didn't start with the Native linguistic icon of wisdom "It is said . . ."

"What does the Sun Dance ceremony tell us about our relationship with Mother Earth?" Mann asked her students.

"To treat her with respect and treasure the gifts she gives," a Native student answered.

Mann nodded and waited while students thought about Sun Dance rituals as a demonstration of glory and thanks.

"How many of you have taken a course in environmental ethics?" Mann asked. Six of the students raised their hands, and Mann nodded toward an Anglo student. "What conclusions did you reach about how to treat the environment?" she asked.

The student paused. The students' responses reflected the quiet, thoughtful approach modeled by their teacher. "We learned that some people think of the land as a resource just there for the utilitarian use of man. Other people think of the Earth as worthwhile in its own sake, with people as the stewards for its resources. But whether you start with an anthropocentric or a biocentric idea of the Earth, you still have a responsibility to be careful how you use it."

The professor smiled as she said, "And Indian people think of the Earth as their mother. So Indian and Anglo people can get to the same conclusion about how to treat the Earth, but we might take different routes to get there."

Ethics serves as a natural bridge across cultures. Every culture has ethical content, explanations, and processes. Every person, regardless of culture or race, is susceptible to the harms that we all want to avoid. The human analogy serves as a connective belief, a basis upon which to build that bridge. The mortality of others and of the others' ability to be harmed is a cross-cultural understanding. Every culture provides basic understandings for how to treat others and the world that sustains us.

However, cultures differ substantially from one another in how they rank goods and evils; they differ in the most fundamental beliefs of the role of human beings in the larger physical world or in transcendental reality. And cultural groups differ widely in their power, politics, and ability to control the expression of their values. Whatever individuals or cultural groups profess, they are often functioning within larger social groups with policies and practices that govern them, like it or not.

This chapter introduces the idea that ethical concerns can serve as a basis for connection between cultural groups when there is a large power differential between the dominant controlling culture and others. Woven through the chapter are suggestions for how ethical understanding and process from nondominant cultures can be incorporated in dealing with ethical issues that transcend cultures.

Western moral philosophy, along with Western political and legal practices, often serves as the basis for developing policy and process to govern cross-cultural communication and action. The assumption that dominant culture provides the only right way to negotiate cultural difference is unjustifiably narrow and limited.

Most often, cross-cultural issues in ethics are recognized only when they arise in the context of multinational business or other inescapable global concern. While this chapter focuses on cultures in nonbusiness contexts, a look at some of the problematic positions taken by some U.S.-based multinational corporations in dealing with other cultures will provide a basis from which to understand the need for alternative approaches.

PROBLEMS OF U.S. BUSINESS IN
INTERNATIONAL CONTEXTS

The first problematic position that U.S.-based corporations have taken in non-U.S. cultures, according to business ethics scholar Richard De George,[1] is that when managers notice that ethical norms differ from place to place, they conclude that the moral responsibility of corporations (or their agents) is to do what is acceptable in the place in which they operate. This position denies the necessity of making normative judgments in determining whose ethics or which ethics is more adequate.

The first problem with this "when in Rome" position is that there is far more moral agreement globally than there is moral disagreement. The Universal Declaration of Human Rights is based on the understanding that all born human beings can be caused harm and ought not be caused harm without justification. What counts as justification, what counts as harm, and what counts as moral causality cannot be clearly understood without context, but the theoretical right of each person to not be caused some harms is universally understood. Indeed, torture and terrorism make sense to perpetrators and victims alike only because of our background of universally understood harms.

This position promotes a mistaken belief that the corporation can act without moral responsibility. But when managers choose to follow local moral norms, this, in itself, is a normative decision.

By way of example, if one holds that it is wrong to kill girl babies in the United States because of their gender, it is also wrong to kill girl babies because of their gender in other parts of the world. The killing of female children is wrong because the children's right to not be caused death without morally adequate justification is a more fundamental right than any culturally based belief or custom. As another example, Americans have recognized for more than 150 years that slavery is wrong. The fact that some powerful classes in some societies enslave or otherwise exploit some part of the population does not provide moral justification for someone who knows better to set aside his or her own correct convictions and participate in the unethical activity.

On the other hand, the desire to impose one's view on others leads to what De George describes as the second problematic position—that of "righteous American."[2] This position insists that American standards be followed elsewhere, regardless of the standards set elsewhere.

The U.S. workday is often divided into units separated by fifteen-minute breaks and a one-hour lunch period. That does not imply that this is how the workday should be envisioned in all settings. The fact that U.S. workplaces are generally secular and do not provide flexibility in the workday for religious expression does not imply that this approach is reasonable in countries with large Muslim populations. Insisting on one's standards can be imperialistic and woefully inappropriate to the setting.

However, the example often used to illustrate the moral permissibility of using different standards in different countries is that of determining the amount to pay employees. Employees in one setting may be paid differently from employees in another. This is true in negotiating wages in Calcutta as compared with Chicago as well as in negotiating wages in Chicago as compared with those to be paid in Clinton, Montana. The difference in degree can ethically reflect different costs of living and different levels of expectations. But the difference of degree (the differential between wages) can become so large that it becomes a difference of kind. If the conventional level of pay amounts to exploitation, it is not ethically acceptable to add to the practice.

In addition, some nations may recognize toxicity or other potential for harms to employees and set regulations to protect employees before other nations develop similar rules. If the corporation recognizes that some material or practice causes unjustifiable risk of harm to employees in one setting, then it follows that it causes unjustifiable risk in all other settings as well, regardless of local law.

Moral managers will provide criteria that distinguish between situations in which the company should assert its own moral standards and when it should yield to local custom or standards. What makes such criteria moral is that the company's flexibility considers the best interest of employees and the community in which it operates, as well as the company's own self-interest.

The third problematic position, described by De George,[3] is that of "naïve immoralist." Instead of asserting that local standards have priority, or that American standards have priority, this position is based on the notion that multinationals need not conform to any culture's ethical standards if doing so is competitively disadvantageous. But acting from a stance of moral neutrality may, in itself, be immoral.

Sometimes acting in a morally permissible way is competitively disadvantageous; sometimes it is not. Sometimes acting in a legally required way is competitively disadvantageous; sometimes it is not. The need for a company to act in a morally permissible way is conceptually different from the need for it to act in an economically advantageous way and the need for it to act in a way that conforms to relevant law. Decision makers have a responsibility to determine corporate actions that are ethically sound, as well as economically and legally sound.

DOMINANT SOCIETY AND INDIGENOUS CULTURE INTERACTIONS

The three problematic positions taken by multinational corporations can be seen in other cross-cultural contexts, such as the historical, as well as contemporary, treatment of indigenous groups by dominant culture. The movement of European settlers into North America provides more than a few examples. The settlers' imposition of their own moral norms without regard to those of the Native American traditions is indicative of the "righteous American." The settlers' willingness to put aside their own standards of fairness and justice as they allowed Native leaders to make trade arrangements based on their contextual naïveté illustrates the "when in Rome" position. The legacy of broken promises to Native populations by European settlers speaks directly to the tendency for the powerful to become "immoralists"—the third position—when dealing with those who are both different and less powerful.

Even contemporary attempts of dominant cultures to mitigate past harms illustrate the problematic positions. Since the 1964 Civil Rights Act, it has been illegal in the United States to discriminate in employment situations or educational environments against people of non-Anglo descent or against women. The process of assimilation treats individuals from minority groups as though they were members of dominant culture. Assimilation, however, is not always just. Indeed, it often provides a contemporary example of the "righteous American" position. Assimilation depends on the assumption that all people are at equal starting points in competing for jobs and that the dominant culture's standards of success are those most appropriate for everyone. Neither assumption is correct for women or cultural and racial minority groups. Many women and non-Anglo persons of both genders in the United States have been disadvantaged in terms of educational backgrounds and experiences as compared with Caucasian males. Purportedly objective testing measures such as IQ tests and entrance exams were found to favor dominant-culture experiences and values. While women and non-Anglo professors brought divergent ideas about successful teaching and learning to universities for decades, student evaluation forms were written so that the questions tended to favor the traditional formal lecture style advanced by white men.

Non-Western cultures provide alternative ways of thinking. Just as Western moral theories differ from one another but have common fundamental assumptions, Native cultures also share universal teachings. These include (1) the practice of daily sanctification; (2) respect, honor, and esteem for all life; (3) honor for the tribal council and acceptance of decisions made through consensus; (4) truthfulness at all times within the tribe; (5) honoring one's guests; (6) empathy with others' feelings and knowing the spirit of the whole; (7) reception of strangers and outsiders with a loving heart; (8) focus on serving others; (9) moderation and balance; (10) knowing both personal well-being and destruction are ultimate outcomes; and (11) following the guidance given to one's heart.[4]

An ethical approach that bridges Anglo cultures and non-Anglo cultures should be based on diversity rather than on assimilation. An ethic of diversity reflects and respects the differences in starting assumptions.

The fundamental moral unit in Native American philosophies is that of the individual in relation to other persons and to spirit and nature. This is in contrast to Western tradition, with the individual as the fundamental moral unit. A cross-cultural ethic based on diversity expects both cultures to bring tools that help create alternative solutions most likely to meet the needs of all.

AN AUSTRALIAN EXAMPLE

What follows is an example, provided by Australian psychologist Jane Selby, of how diversity between cultures can be accepted in cross-cultural instruction.[5] Here is Dr. Selby's story:

Australia's indigenous peoples are thought to hold knowledge quite distinct from those developed by Western colonizers.[6] *Yet Western training and resources are recognized by indigenous as well as white leaders as a crucial feature in successful attempts to redress the effects of dispossession and disadvantage which indigenous peoples continue to live under.*[7] *The following will illustrate the awkwardness, as well as the potential, as these somewhat opposing contexts come together.*

In the late 1990s, I developed and delivered a course that aimed at training indigenous mental health workers. The course was used, among other things, as a stand-alone certificate for those who were already active in mental health work in communities. The course aimed at providing on-site education for indigenous health care workers so they would be better prepared to respond to community needs.

Some of the students were experienced traditional healers open to dialogue with Western knowledge. One, whom I'll call Trevor, was interested in hearing about the whole setting up of the course and came to know about some of the (inevitable) glitches, which I had had to manage. For example, I convened a reference group of local stakeholders to oversee the planning, to be kept informed, and to contribute as they thought appropriate. This group comprised mainly local indigenous representatives but also some nonindigenous professionals, including a government departmental official. This person held strong views about how mental health workers should be trained, including what priorities should be set for them to follow. He was experienced as "high handed" by the reference group, a group which itself represented a range of conflicting points of view and agendas. My one-to-one discussions with him reflected his dissatisfaction with how the training was being planned. I experienced his behavior as his wishing the training to fail.

At one point, while I was discussing this person informally with colleagues and friends, Trevor joined us, listened for a while, then turned to me and seemed to look in and through my eyes. He said quietly but very clearly, "Do you want him to have a heart attack?"

Was this meant to be funny or not? Actually, I felt frightened. Then I felt tempted. Then I mumbled, "No."

I had a formal relationship with Trevor, the traditional healer, and he seemed serious. I had already talked with him about his work and about the extraordinary capabilities he talked about having gained from his father. Other members of his community provided, from time to time, descriptions of Trevor's status and power. This offer to remove someone who is an obstacle to a good end, I suggest, is not so unique, and those who have worked with indigenous communities may well have witnessed or become involved with incidents (or potential outcomes) that challenge our epistemological and ontological complacencies.

While the course thus started under something of a cloud, in fact, the few weeks of class went well, as did the four weeks of placements for the participants as mental health workers. Toward the end of the course, students prepared for a major assessment.

Each student, individually or in small groups, presented a case. Their guidelines were standard enough: details of referral, an assessment, a plan, an intervention, and an outcome. The assessment was based less on some form of clinical correctness than it was on demonstrated capacity to think about the case and to demonstrate skill learned in the work done together.

It was Trevor's turn to be assessed. He stood up.

"Well, there's this man at the clinic and the nurses have asked me to help."

The man had talked about someone outside the room who was trying to kill him. The white nurses assessed him as delusional and paranoiac, and they felt unable to help. There was no Western medic available in the remote community, so they called in Trevor, the traditional healer.

Trevor arrived. He knew the man. First, he clarified with the patient his multiple classifications of kin, clan, and marital linkages. This was because of the importance of understanding the man's "positionings" within the community. So it was that Trevor worked out his diagnosis. He helped the patient identify who he felt to be outside the door of the room. Knowledge of the man's "positionings" allowed Trevor to engage the man in conversation regarding the configuration of jealousy, covertness, and complexities of payback. He understood the patient's fear of the strength of the murderous powers he felt were directed at him.

Trevor then called together the appropriate men from the community. Together, they went to the Place. Trevor cannot tell us what "the Place" means or what they do there. It is either secret knowledge or special knowledge that cannot be conveyed in this setting, a group of students with their lecturer from the university. But the upshot of what happened at the Place is that Trevor now knew exactly what was required to break the murderous hold that the individual had over his patient.

"I knew then what to do, but," as he recounted the ordeal, he looked troubled and weary, "I also knew there was risk involved to myself."

Trevor decided to proceed. He confronted the man with murderous intentions toward his patient and was able to resolve the situation. The patient stopped seeing the death-bearing man at the door; he rested, recovered, and went home cured.

Moving away from how I actually reviewed Trevor's work, which did, indeed, have an assessment, plan, intervention, and outcome, I want to highlight two points. First, I was pleased to hear Trevor talk of the risk to himself in his clinical work. While in Western culture, mental health workers may talk of burnout and even of some of the material threats from patients, the risks involved in clinical work are undertheorized in the dominant culture. But it's not only clinicians who feel vulnerable in their work. Most of us in the course of our work, domestic life, and play have the challenging task of distinguishing, then owning or attributing to others, emotional states, which have real implications for ourselves and those around us.

When I am doing my work, I ask myself, do I feel uneasy because I had a row with my spouse last night, or has that patient conveyed to me something that transports me into a series of traumatic flashbacks? Trevor did not elaborate on the risks that he encountered other than to convey the internal and private nature of conflict. In doing so, he brought to the surface an element often ignored in the Western professional perspective. It hardly matters if we can attribute reason to the clinician's feeling of risk. When a caregiver feels at risk, he or she has the responsibility to respond both to self and to client.

The experience with Trevor touches on the risks in the processes of understanding and interventions, risks which Western-trained researchers and clinicians may try to ignore. Thus in the "heart attack" example, had I said "Yes" to Trevor's invitation, I might have lost my security blanket of Western rationality and personal moral integrity, sold my soul to the devil, and entered ways of thinking and being where I would have no roadmap. In Trevor's clinical account, he described some danger of intervention, reminiscent of how, in clinical and research training, we take great care to protect and divorce our own experiences and reactions from the matter at hand, precisely to defend against dangers. In clinical settings, psychologists in the Western tradition manage to standardize and test and provide programs for patients all at an arm's length.

Work with indigenous cultures reminds Western workers that reality can be quite different. Reflective clinicians, teachers, and researchers allow the experience of risk and discomfort to produce insight for us and for those with whom we work.

Selby's approach illustrates how respect allows indigenous and Anglo facilitators and participants to become partners who can learn from one another's cultures.

This approach can also be seen in an example that reaches beyond shared professional interest.

A U.S.–NATIVE AMERICAN
BRIDGE ACROSS CULTURES

The Flathead Indian Reservation in Northwestern Montana is home to the Confederated Salish and Kootenai Tribes. The tribes consist of a confederation of Salish and Pend d'Orielles Tribes and the Kootenai, an individual tribe. Of the approximately 6,800 enrolled tribal members, approximately 4,000 live on or near the reservation. There are also Indians on the reservation who are enrolled with other tribes. But with more than 21,000 non-Indians living on the reservation, the non-Indian population outnumbers the Native population four to one.

The reservation is located in the western part of Montana on the western slope of the Rocky Mountains. It is a beautiful area of fertile plains surrounded by rugged tree-covered slopes and high snow-capped peaks. Its exterior borders encompass 1,250,000 acres. The northern border is Flathead Lake, the largest freshwater lake west of the Mississippi River. It is 27 miles long and 26 miles wide, covering 188 square miles.[8]

The reservation bridges two major population centers. The first is Missoula, which is the largest community in western Montana. It is located approximately 20 miles from the reservation's southern border. Kalispell, the second largest community in the area, is located approximately 25 miles from the reservation's northern border.[9]

The land in Northwestern Montana is appealing to people interested in hunting, fishing, or other outdoor activities. Area real estate agents often show land or homes to potential buyers from out of state who don't understand what it means to buy land on a reservation or what it means to live on land that is an Indian sovereign nation. In the interest of making sales, few agents take the time to educate these potential land or homeowners. Non-Native property owners often fail to understand why their hunting and fishing are regulated in ways that the Native citizens' are not. Most non-Native newcomers are surprised to learn that under an agreement with the state and local governments, the tribes may handle crimes committed by Indian defendants within the reservation but may choose to refer felony offenses to the state, while non-Native people charged with crimes are automatically turned over to state authorities.[10]

One important offshoot of Native sovereign nations' freedom to deal with crimes in a traditional way is that Native cultures can choose to use traditional methods not open to the dominant culture. For example, in January 2000, the Navajo Nation eliminated jail time and fines as the punishment for seventy-nine offenses. Instead, they use the traditional concept of "nalyeeh," which allows those who have been hurt, along with their advocates, to confront the person accused of an offense along with his or her relatives. This traditional method of justice achieves two goals not possible through the dominant-society process: first, the process focuses on the effects of the crime; next, it keeps victims in the center of the process.

The Flathead Reservation was opened to settlement by non-Indians in 1910 by President Howard Taft. By the 1990s, the Indians had become a minority on their own reservation. The communities, including school boards, city councils, city governments, and the majority of businesses, are non-Indian controlled or owned. Tensions developed on the reservation because of differing perceptions of Indian rights to control the land and those who reside upon it. Non-Native residents tended to think of the reservation as a gift from the Federal government to the Indians, not understanding that the tribes are occupying just a very small percentage of their traditional lands.

Indian and non-Indian citizens of the Flathead formed a community action group, Neighbors, in 1993 to address the tensions that were often classified as clashes between Native and non-Native perspectives or values. The organization is intended to "promote communication and cooperation between and among tribal and non-tribal people and institutions on the Reservation." According to the group's brochure,

> Our group accepts and supports the historical and constitutional right of the Confederated Salish and Kootenai Tribes to govern themselves and to manage their own affairs. We recognize and honor all the distinctive cultures that contribute to the rich diversity of the Flathead Reservation.[11]

Neighbors prepared a position paper on tribal sovereignty in 1996 to help non-Native local residents understand this important principle of tribal control. According to the position paper, "We believe that clarity on the issue of tribal sovereignty is essential if tribal and non-tribal people are to overcome polarization and work together effectively to meet the many challenges that face us as a community."[12]

Some of the most important components of that paper include information on interpretation of treaties: "Ambiguities in treaties must be decided in favor of Indian claims. Treaties must be interpreted as the Indians would have understood them at the time of the signing. Treaties must be construed liberally in favor of the Indians."[13]

The group also seeks to help non-Native residents understand and practice incorporating Native lifestyles and approaches to problem solving. Even if Indians are given added weight in the legal interpretation of treaties, Neighbors reminds us that the treaties and the legal system of interpretation are non-Native ways of dealing with conflict.

Neighbors uses a system called "formal consensus" for their own decision-making process and offers workshops for the community in the process. This system is close to traditional Native ways of dealing with conflict.

According to one member,

> Consensus fosters an environment in which everyone is respected and all contributions are valued. Voting encourages competition, often without regard to others'

concerns. Since its goal is the winning of most votes, using majority rule risks alienation and apathy within the group.

Formal Consensus provides a clearly defined structure so that even the most complicated decision can be made more calmly and timely. But to accomplish this, it also requires training and discipline. Formal Consensus is nonviolent, democratic, based upon the group's principles, better in larger groups, better when everyone participates, not inherently time-consuming, and cannot be secretly disrupted.[14]

Generally speaking, the values of more powerful Euro-based cultures have been imposed on those from divergent cultures in matters of mutual interest, often to the detriment of the less powerful culture and always indicating a lack of respect for the values of the non-Anglo culture. Principles that emerge from a synthesis of Anglo-based and indigenous cultures have shown to be respectful of both groups and to provide creative alternatives not found when using nothing other than the values of the powerful. Following are examples:

1. Recognize common need. When people of different cultures inhabit a shared setting, whether an Indian reservation or the world, it is helpful to begin with a recognition that all persons share common interests in avoiding harm and in preserving the environmental context in which people live.
2. Begin agreement by recognizing what both groups consider to be intolerable. Different cultural groups may have different priorities or desires. However, a starting point for agreement is mutual acceptance of what is not a tolerable outcome for either. Agreement on what is morally prohibited is often easier to reach than agreement on what is morally ideal.
3. Value diversity over assimilation. Assimilation assumes there is one right way to which everyone should try to conform. Diversity recognizes that alternative approaches can yield an unexpected synthesis of both. Thus, diversity allows a broad set of standards for success.
4. Listen to and value the nondominant culture. Neither cultural reference is always right or all wrong, but persons from nondominant cultures may have ways of communicating that are different from the linear, rationally based Western style of developing and defending conclusions. If one is listening solely for the merits of the case, one is likely to miss the rich nuances involved with a more narrative or stream-of-consciousness approach to thinking about issues.
5. In those instances in which everyone's needs cannot be met, favor the most vulnerable. Favoring the most vulnerable, which is usually the nondominant culture, includes the perspective that there are more ways that the needs of dominant culture can be met. Favoring the least powerful mitigates for past harms.

It is easy for Anglos, comfortable in dominant cultures, to deny that there may be important cultural differences in interactions with those from non-Euro cultures, in interactions with women, and in interactions with people with disabilities. It is easiest to assume that everyone thinks and feels "the way that I do." But what is easiest is not likely to bridge cultures. Better to start a conversation, negotiation, or confrontation with the understanding that each brings a unique toolbox for dealing with the matter at hand. Sharing the tools provides the most inclusive way of reaching decisions together.

NOTES

1. Richard T. De George, *Competing with Integrity in International Business* (New York: Oxford University Press, 1993), 9–22.

2. De George, *Competing*, 9.

3. De George, *Competing*, 17.

4. Thomas Cooper, *A Time before Deception: Truth in Communication, Culture and Ethics* (Santa Fe, NM: Clear Light Publishers, 1998).

5. This essay was written for this publication but is also discussed in Jane Selby, "Disruptions of Identity: Dynamics of Working across Indigenous Differences," *Qualitative Studies in Education* 17, no. 1 (2004): 143–156; and Jane Selby, "Discomfort in Research: Theorising from Dynamics across Indigenous Settings," in *Theoretical Advances in Psychology*, ed. N. Stephenson, H. L. Radtke, R. J. Jorna, and H. J. Stam (Amsterdam: Kluwer, 2003), 358–367.

6. M. G. Wessells and D. Bretherton, "Psychological Reconciliation: National and International Perspectives," *Australian Psychologist* 35, no. 2 (2000): 100–108.

7. Jane Selby, "Cross-Cultural Research in Health Psychology: Illustrations from Australia," in *Qualitative Health Psychology: Theories and Methods*, ed. M. Murray and K. Chamerlain (London: Sage, 1999), 164–180.

8. Char-Koosta News, "Confederated Salish and Kootenai Tribes," www.cskt.org (accessed March 17, 2006).

9. www.uchsc.edu/ai/hni/salis/salishos.htm (accessed March 17, 2004).

10. "Tribal Sovereignty (1880–1887)," www.skc.edu/netbook/06-tribal_sovereignty .htm (accessed March 16, 2006).

11. Neighbors information card, unpublished.

12. Neighbors draft position paper on tribal sovereignty, February 1996, unpublished.

13. Neighbors draft.

14. C. T. Lawrence Butler, "Consensus Revisited," *Neighbors News* (May 1994): 2.

Glossary

The terms included reflect stipulated meanings used in this book and may not fit conventional usage.

absolutism—a style of moral judgment that begins with the belief that rules are rigid and always hold (e.g., don't lie no matter what).

aggregate good—the good of the whole, which may be different from the good of the individuals added together. Mill's utilitarianism is often misunderstood to be a quantified theory (the greatest good for the greatest number, the least harm for the smallest number). He clarifies in chapter 3 of *Utilitarianism* that our individual happiness rests on the health of the whole community, that achieving happiness is not a struggle between rivals but rather a recognition of what contributes to the overall happiness in an aggregate rather than quantified sense.

analogy, argument by—an argument by analogy concludes that since situation A and situation B are similar in relevant ways, the best answer in B will be the same as the best answer in A.

applied ethics—the application of an ethical theory or system to real-life issues.

argument—a technical term to describe the structure of reasoning that includes one or more premises and a conclusion.

authority, appeal to—using a person as a reason for holding a certain view. Some appeals to authority, based on expertise, are good reasons for holding a view (e.g., the weatherperson said that a hurricane is heading this way). Other appeals to authority do not provide good reasons for holding a view (e.g., my boss said I should do this, so I will even though I think it's wrong).

autonomous—internally directed.

bandwagon—a fallacious way of reasoning that rests on the idea that a choice is ethically acceptable because "everyone" holds that view.

begging the question—a fallacious way of reasoning in which the support of the conclusion is just another way of stating the conclusion (e.g., the mother who killed her children should be found not guilty by reason of insanity because she'd have to be crazy to do something like that); begging the question also occurs when a normative question is recast as a question of economics, law, or opinion.

cogent—an argument that has true and complete premises and a probably true conclusion but lacks strict deductive validity; an argument that lacks cogency does not include relevant information or worthy counterarguments.

conclusion—the statement at the end of the argument that states what the listener should accept.

consequentialism—a method of ethical decision making that determines the moral permissibility of an action based on actual or predictable outcomes.

contradiction—the logical claim that counters a proposition. ~A is the contradiction to A. The contradiction to "abortion in some cases is morally permitted" is "abortion is never morally permitted."

contrary—the logical claim that there is middle ground in what is presented as an either-or situation. For example, if an editor says that the choice is whether or not to print a questionable photograph, she may be ignoring possible contrary actions. See **false dilemma**.

deduction—the logical claim that the conclusion of an argument necessarily follows from its premises.

deontology—a method of ethical decision making that determines the moral permissibility of an action based on an analysis of the agent's role-related responsibilities and/or intentionality, often without regard to the consequences of a specific act (e.g., it is right that teachers flunk students who perform poorly because it is the teacher's duty to give students the grades they earn).

descriptive ethics—an analysis of human conduct that details how people *do* behave in regard to one another (rather than how they *should* behave).

duty—the special responsibility associated with a particular profession/occupation or societal role (doctors have unique duties; so do journalists, students, and parents). The duty of an individual or group includes description of how that responsibility is unique and essential to the legitimate social role. See **role-related responsibility**.

duty-based ethics—see **deontology**.

ethicist—a word made up by news media to describe a certain kind of source.

ethics—the discipline that looks at how people do and should act in regard to subjects of moral worth (from the Greek *ethike*, meaning custom). See **morality**.

exceptionism—a style of moral judgment that is universal but not absolute. Exceptionists believe there are justified exceptions to universal moral rules.

false dilemma—the presentation of alternatives in a dichotomous way (e.g., "either print the story or don't" is a false dilemma; there are many other choices: print later, print some, print differently).

fatalistic relativism—a refusal to engage in ethical analysis characterized by the speaker's unwillingness to judge another person's actions or motivations.

fundamental moral unit (FMU)—the primary basis for moral consideration. In classical Western ethics, the FMU is the individual person; in some feminist critiques, the FMU is the relationship among people; in some non-Western and indigenous philosophies, the FMU is the system that sustains connections between humans and other natural and transcendental entities.

generalizable—the ability to apply a rule or an exception to others who are similarly situated.

harm—what all rational people want to avoid for themselves, unless they have what they think is a good reason for wanting it. Direct harms include death, pain, disability, and being deprived of freedom or pleasure. Indirect harms include being deceived or cheated and having people break promises, break the law, or neglect duties toward you. What is irrational to want for oneself is immoral to cause to another.

heteronomous—externally directed.

human analogy—the understanding that all competent human beings have that other human beings can suffer harms and want other people to refrain from causing them to suffer those harms.

ideal—how we would like people to act but don't think they *have* to act: an ideal action is one that is morally encouraged but not morally required.

idealism—the assumption that desirable outcomes can be obtained without causing harms.

impartiality—a requirement for minimalist morality that requires that moral agents avoid causing harm without adequate justification to all people.

induction—a type of argument in which the conclusion is based on premises that note instances and probability. The best inductive arguments are those that are based on the most instances (e.g., my heart has been beating for more than fifty years; it will continue to beat today). But as that example shows, conclusions based on many instances will turn out to be wrong if other data that make the argument cogent (such as mortality) are ignored.

irrationality—the key to a system of morality. It is irrational to want harm without reason. It is immoral to cause what it is irrational to want.

judgment—deciding what is morally required, prohibited, permitted, or encouraged in a particular situation.

justification—how one explains that behavior that causes harm is permitted in a particular case. A questionable act such as lying is strongly justified if all rational impartial persons *could* advocate lying in situations of that kind (i.e., it would not be irrational to advocate it). The questionable act is not justified if no rational impartial persons could advocate lying in situations that have the same morally relevant features. It is weakly justified if a rational impartial person could go either way.

law—a system of rules different from ethics: the scope of law includes only what is enforceable; the scope of morality excludes whatever causes unjustified harms.

minimalist morality—systems that describe only those behaviors that are morally prohibited.

mixed formalism—a contemporary style of ethical reasoning that uses elements from different classical ethical theories, recognizing that different classical theories may prioritize different, but equally important, morally relevant features. Mixed formalists create decision-making processes that include review of features from different theories.

moral agent—a competent, rational, conscious adult who is voluntarily choosing an action or inaction.

moral community—all human beings between birth and death; those deserving of moral protections equal to what all others deserve. It is morally prohibited to cause a member of the moral community unjustified harm without good reason.

moral development—a theory that describes moral sophistication and the steps that one follows in reaching moral sophistication.

moral system—the structure that both describes how people *do* act in regard to one another and prescribes how people *should* act in regard to one another. A moral system differentiates among behaviors that are morally prohibited, those that are morally permitted, those that are morally required, and those that are morally encouraged.

morality—see **ethics** (from the Latin *moralis*, meaning custom).

morally relevant difference—a difference that shows why one entity deserves to be treated differently from another in similar circumstances. For example, children may be deprived of some freedoms for their own protection because of their age and perceived inability to take full responsibility for their actions. This is a morally relevant difference between children and adults.

normative ethics—arguments leading to the conclusion of how people *should* behave in regard to one another (as differentiated from how they *do* behave).

objective—having reality or truth-value external to the judgment of individuals. Torture of innocent children is objectively wrong as it is a cause of unjustified harms.

permitted—behavior that is within the bounds of the moral system. It is morally permitted to act in any way that does not cause others unjustified harms.

practical ethics—the study of how people *do* act and how they *should* act in regard to others and in regard to subjects of moral worth.

professional ethics—the study of how people *do* perform and how they *should* perform job-related duties.

prohibited—behavior that is not morally permitted. It is morally prohibited to act in ways that cause others to suffer unjustified harms.

rationality—1. the inverse of irrationality; 2. the ability to know that oneself and others can be harmed, the ability to recognize harms as such, and the ability to understand that questionable action requires justification.

reason—an appeal to benefit for oneself or others. If one has a *reason* for doing something, it is because the agent believes that someone will benefit.

relativism—the belief that there are no universal moral rules.

required—behavior that an agent *must* do. People are morally required to meet their role-related responsibilities and to avoid causing unjustifiable harms to others.

rights—what follows from being a member of the moral community. Subjects of moral worth have a *right* to not be caused unjustified harms.

role-related responsibility—the unique duty associated with one of a person's multiple societal roles.

rule—how we expect people to act unless they have a good reason for doing otherwise; people are blameworthy if they violate a rule.

slippery slope—the fallacy of deriving an unacceptable conclusion from incremental steps. For example, if we allow abortion, then we'll allow the killing of newborns; once that happens, we will allow the killing of all who cannot defend themselves. Therefore, we should not allow abortion.

soundness—a judgment about the quality of an argument. An argument is sound if it has true premises and a true conclusion and if it is valid. Arguments in ethics will rarely have logical validity and thus will rarely be sound, in a strict logical sense. However, the goal is to avoid fallacious reasoning and produce as strong and cogent an argument as possible.

stewardship—the voluntary assumption of responsibility for a subject of moral worth.

straw man—the fallacious method of reasoning that involves constructing a very weak counterargument to the position one holds.

subjective—not objective; having reality or truth-value only in regard to what people think. A subjective way of thinking can lead to the following fallacious conclusion: If I think something is wrong, it is wrong. My thinking makes it so.

subjects of moral worth—entities outside of the moral community that deserve moral consideration (e.g., human corpses, human fetuses, some animals, the environment, art, and culture are subjects of moral worth). They ought not be caused harm without good reason but are not of value equal to those in the moral community.

teleology—the set of moral theories that justifies questionable actions by appeal to an ultimate outcome—the ultimate outcome could be expected good consequences, or it could be self-actualization of the agent.

theory—the foundation that supports a system; by way of analogy, a grammatical theory explains how and why a grammar system works.

universal—applies to everyone in similar circumstances.

utilitarianism—theories that justify choices by appeal to the greatest good or the greatest aggregate good for the community (or the least aggregate harm for the community).

validity—a judgment about the structure of an argument if it has true premises and true conclusion.

values—expressions of what people desire or want to avoid. Ethical primary values articulate what people want to avoid or seek for their own good. Rankings of values differ among people. There are also aesthetic and religious values that are not necessarily connected with ethics.

virtue ethics—the set of moral theories that appeals to what one's moral hero might do. The agent, rather than the act, is judged. One uses virtue ethics to consider how to be the kind of person who promotes good and prevents harm.

Bibliography

Ammon, Theodore G. 1992. "Teachers Should Disclose Their Moral Commitments." In *Moral Education and the Liberal Arts*, edited by Michael Mitias, 163–161. New York: Greenwood.

Anderson, Gustaf. 1990. "Why Formal Ethical Theory Ought to Be Taught in Professional Ethics Courses." *APA Newsletter on Teaching Philosophy* (Fall): 67–71.

Applebaum, B. 2002. "Teaching Applied Ethics, Critical Theory, and 'Having to Brush One's Teeth.'" *Teaching Philosophy* 25(1): 27–40.

Aristotle. *Eudemian Ethics*. Translated by Michael Woods, 2nd ed. New York: Oxford University Press, 1992.

———. *Nicomachean Ethics*. Translated by Martin Ostwald. Upper Saddle River, NJ: Prentice Hall, 1999.

Badaracco, Joseph L. 1998. "The Discipline of Building Character." *Harvard Business Review* (March/April): 115–124.

Baetz, Mark, and Auleen Carson. 1999. "Ethical Dilemmas in Teaching about Ethical Dilemmas: Obstacle or Opportunity?" *Teaching Business Ethics* 3: 1–12.

Baier, Annette C. 1985. "What Do Women Want in a Moral Theory?" *Nous* 19(1): 53–63.

Barash, David P. 2001. "Kant Isn't Just for Kindergartners," *Chronicle of Higher Education*, June 8, B5.

Belenky, M. F., B. M. Clinchy, N. R. Goldberger, and J. M. Tarule. 1986. *Women's Ways of Knowing: The Development of Self, Voice, and Mind*. New York: Basic.

Benhabib, Seyla. 1992. *Situating the Self: Gender, Community and Postmodernism in Contemporary Ethics*. Cambridge, UK: Polity.

Bensen, Robert. 2001. *Children of the Dragonfly: Native American Voices on Child Custody and Education*. Tucson: University of Arizona Press.

Bergem, Trygve. 1990. "The Teacher as Moral Agent." *Journal of Moral Education* 19(2): 88–100.

Biggins, David R. 1999. "Research in Aboriginal Health: Priorities, Ethics and Philosophy." *New Doctor* (Summer): 28–30.

Birch, Mary, Deni Elliott, and Mary Trankel. 1999. "Black and White and Shades of Gray: A Portrait of the Ethical Professor." *Ethics & Behavior* 9(3): 243–261.

Birkhead, Douglas. 1997. "Should Professional Competence Be Taught as Ethical?" *Journal of Mass Media Ethics* 12(4): 211–220.

Blum, Lawrence. 1997. "Multicultural Education as Values Education." *Harvard Project on Schooling and Children: Working Papers*. Cambridge: Harvard Project on Schooling and Children.

———. 1998. "Can We Talk? Interracial Dialogue in the University Classroom." *Change* (November/December): 27–37.

Bok, Derek. 1982. "The Moral Development of Students." In *Beyond the Ivory Tower*, 116–135. Cambridge: Harvard University Press.

———. 1988. "Can Ethics Be Taught?" *Ethics: Easier Said than Done* 1(1): 9–15.

Bok, Sissela. 1978. *Lying: Moral Choice in Public and Private Life*. New York: Vintage.

———. 1988. "Kant's Arguments in Support of the Maxim 'Do What Is Right Though the World Should Perish.'" *Argumentation* 2: 7–25.

Bomstad, Linda. 1995. "Advocating Procedural Neutrality." *Teaching Philosophy* 18(3): 197–210.

Boss, Judith A. 1994. "The Effect of Community Service Work on the Moral Development of College Ethics Students." *Journal of Moral Education* 23(2): 183–198.

Bowie, Norman E. 1985. "Applied Philosophy: Its Meaning and Justification." *Journal of Applied Philosophy* 1(1): 1–18.

Brod, Harry. 1986. "Philosophy Teaching as Intellectual Affirmative Action." *Teaching Philosophy* 9(1): 53–61.

Callahan, Daniel. 1980. "Goals in the Teaching of Ethics." In *Ethics Teaching in Higher Education*, edited by Daniel Callahan and Sissela Bok, 61–80. New York: Plenum.

Callahan, Joan C. 1997. "From the 'Applied' to the Practical: Teaching Ethics for Use." In *In the Socratic Tradition: Essays on Teaching Philosophy*, edited by Tziporah Kasachkoff, 57–69. Lanham, MD: Rowman & Littlefield.

Caplan, Arthur. 1980. "Evaluation and the Teaching of Ethics." In *Ethics Teaching in Higher Education*, edited by Daniel Callahan and Sissela Bok, 133–150. New York: Plenum.

Carr, David. 1991. *Educating the Virtues: An Essay on the Philosophical Psychology of Moral Development and Education*. London: Routledge.

———. 1999. "Professional Education and Professional Ethics." *Journal of Applied Philosophy* 16(1): 33–46.

Carson, Thomas L. 1988. "Who Are We to Judge?" *Teaching Philosophy* 11(1): 33–44.

Chadwick, Ruth, Dan Callahan, and Peter Singer. 1997. *Encyclopedia of Applied Ethics*. London: Academic Press.

Christians, Clifford, and Michael Traber. 1997. *Communication Ethics and Universal Values*. Thousand Oaks, CA: Sage.

Colby, Anne. 2000. "The Place of Moral Interpretation and Habit in Moral Development." *Human Development* 43: 161–164.

Cole, Eve Browning. 1994. "Women, Slaves, and 'Love of Toil' in Aristotle's Moral Philosophy." In *Critical Feminist Readings in Plato and Aristotle*, edited by Bat-Ami Bar On. New York: State University of New York Press.

Connor, W. Robert. 1999. "Moral Knowledge in the Modern University." *Ideas* 6(1): 56–67.

Cooper, Thomas W. 1998. *A Time before Deception: Truth in Communication, Culture and Ethics*. Santa Fe, NM: Clear Light Publications.

De George, Richard T. 1986. "Corporate Responsibility and the Social Audit." In *Business Ethics*, 2nd ed., 151–175. New York: MacMillan.

————. 1993. *Competing with Integrity in International Business*. New York: Oxford University Press.

Donaldson, Thomas. 1996. "Values in Tension: When Is Different Just Different and When Is Different Wrong?" *Harvard Business Review* (September/October): 101–110.

Donovan, Aine. 1999. "Celestial Navigation, with a Moral Compass." *Journal for a Just and Caring Education* 5(3): 285–297.

Egonsson, Dan. 1997. "Kant's Vegetarianism." *Journal of Value Inquiry* 31: 473–483.

Elliott, Deni. 1985. "Education: Avoiding Indoctrination through Ethics Instruction." *SPJ/SDX Ethics Report*.

————. 1991. "Moral Development Theories and the Teaching of Ethics." *Journalism Educator* (Autumn): 18–24.

————. 1997. "The Great Hanshin Earthquake and the Ethics of Intervention: A Case-Study in International and Intercultural Communication." In *Ethics in Intercultural and International Communication*, edited by Fred L. Casmir, 43–58. Mawhaw, NJ: Erlbaum.

————. 1997. "Universal Values and Moral Development Theories." In *Communication Ethics and Universal Values*, edited by C. Christians and M. Traber, 68–83. Thousand Oaks, CA: Sage

————. 2001. "A New Warp and Weft in the Classroom." *Chronicle of Higher Education*, July 6, B5.

Elliott, Deni, and Judy E. Stern. 1996. "Evaluating Teaching and Students' Learning of Academic Research Ethics." *Science and Engineering Ethics* 2: 345–366.

Enright, Robert D., Elizabeth A. Gassin, and Ching-Ru Wu. 1992. "Forgiveness: A Developmental View." *Journal of Moral Education* 21(2): 99–115.

Esquith, Stephen L. 1988. "How Neutral Is Discussion?" *Teaching Philosophy* 11(3): 89–104.

Euben, J. Peter. 1981. "Philosophy and the Professions." *Democracy* 1(2): 112–127.

Frankena, William K. 1958. "Toward a Philosophy of Moral Education." *Harvard Educational Review* 28(4): 300–313.

Gatens, Moira. 1991. *The Feminist Critique of Philosophy*. Bloomington: Indiana University Press.

Gert, Bernard. 1992. "Morality, Moral Theory, and Applied and Professional Ethics." *Professional Ethics Journal* 1(1/2): 5–24.

————. 1995. "Morality vs. Slogans." In *Morality in Criminal Justice*, edited by Daryl Close and Nicholas Meier, 51–60. Belmont, CA: Wadsworth.

————. 2001. "Avoiding Moral Cynicism." *Teaching Ethics Journal* 1(1): 1–17.

————. 2004. *Common Morality: Deciding What to Do*. New York: Oxford University Press.

————. 2005. *Morality: Its Nature and Justification*. Rev. ed. New York: Oxford University Press.

Gibney, Mark P. 1999. "Missing the Forest for the Trees." *The Humanist* (May/June): 19–22.

Gilbertson, Mark O. 1998. "A 'Meeting-of-Minds' Discussion as a Final Exam in History of Philosophy." In *In the Socratic Tradition: Essays on Teaching Philosophy*, edited by Tziporah Kasachkoff, 181–184. Lanham, MD: Rowman & Littlefield.

Gilligan, Carol, and John Michael Murphy. 1979. "Development from Adolescence to

Adulthood: The Philosopher and the Dilemma of the Fact." In *Intellectual Development beyond Childhood*, edited by D. Kunn, 85–98. San Francisco: Jossey-Bass.

———. 1982. "New Maps of Development: New Visions of Maturity." *American Journal of Orthopsychiatry* 52(2): 199–212.

———. 1982. *In a Different Voice*. Cambridge: Harvard University Press.

———. 1998. "Remembering Larry." *Journal of Moral Education* 7(2): 125–140.

Ginsburg, Robert. 1992. "The Humanities, Moral Education, and the Contemporary World." In *Moral Education and the Liberal Arts*, edited by Michael H. Mitias, 29–44. New York: Greenwood.

Goldman, Michael. 1994. "Why?" *Teaching Philosophy* 17(4): 45–52.

Goodlad, J. I., R. Soder, and K. A. Sirotnik. 1990. *The Moral Dimensions of Teaching*. San Francisco: Jossey-Bass.

Gouinlock, James. 1992. "Moral Pluralism, Intellectual Virtue, and Academic Culture." In *Moral Education and the Liberal Arts*, edited by Michael H. Mitias, 77–92. New York: Greenwood.

Gould, J. B. 2002. "Better Hearts." *Teaching Applied Virtue Ethics* 25(1): 1–26.

Gracyk, Theodore A. 1998. "A Critical Thinking Portfolio." In *In the Socratic Tradition: Essays on Teaching Philosophy*, edited by Tziporah Kasachkoff, 153–159. Lanham, MD: Rowman & Littlefield.

Graham, P. Tony, and Paul C. Cline. 1980. "The Case Method: A Basic Teaching Approach." *Theory into Practice* 19(2): 112–116.

Green, Thomas F. 1966. "Teaching, Acting and Behaving." In *Philosophy and Education*, 2nd ed., edited by Israel Scheffler, 115–135. Boston: Allyn & Bacon.

Grinde, Donald A., and Bruce E. Johansen. 1995. *Ecocide of Native America*. Santa Fe, NM: Clear Light Publishers.

Groenhout, Ruth. 1998. "The Virtue of Care: Aristotelian Ethics and Contemporary Ethics of Care." In *Feminist Interpretations of Aristotle*, edited by Cynthia A. Freeland, 171–200. University Park: Pennsylvania State University Press.

Hansen, Abby. 1991. "Establishing a Teaching/Learning Contract." In *Education for Judgment*, edited by C. Roland Christensen, David A. Garvin, and Ann Sweet, 123–135. Cambridge: Harvard Business School Press.

Hanson, Karen. 1996. "Between Apathy and Advocacy: Teaching and Modeling Ethical Reflection." In *Ethical Dimensions of College and University Teaching, No. 66*, edited by Linc Fisch, 33–36. San Francisco: Jossey-Bass.

Held, Virginia. 1990. "Feminist Transformations of Moral Theory." *Philosophy and Phenomenological Research* (Fall supplement): 321–344.

Hennessey, John W., and Bernard Gert. 1985. "Moral Rules and Moral Ideals: A Useful Distinction in Business and Professional Practice." *Journal of Business Ethics* 4: 105–115.

Hobson, Peter, and Adrian Walsh. 1998. "The Pedagogic Value of General Moral Principles in Professional Ethics." *Professional Ethics* 6(3/4): 33–48.

Hoffman, W. Michael, Judith Brown Kamm, Robert E. Frederick, and Edward S. Petry. 1994. *Emerging Global Business Ethics*. Westport, CT: Quorum.

Jaggar, Alison M. 2000. "Feminism and Moral Philosophy." *APA Newsletter on Feminism and Philosophy* (Spring): 200–206.

Jennings, Bruce, James Lindemann Nelson, and Erik Parens. 1993. *Values on Campus:*

Ethics and Values Programs in the Undergraduate Curriculum. New York: Hastings Center.

Johnson, W. Brad, and Nancy Nelson. 1999. "Mentor-Protege Relationships in Graduate Training: Some Ethical Concerns." *Ethics & Behavior* 9(3): 189–210.

Josephson Institute. 1989. "A Catalogue of Ethical Transgressions." *Ethics: Easier Said than Done* 2(1): 42.

Kant, Immanuel. 1964. *Groundwork for the Metaphysics of Morals*. Translated by H. J. Paton. New York: Harper.

———. 1980. *Lectures on Ethics*. Translated by Louis Infield. Indianapolis, IN: Hackett.

Larrabee, Mary Jeanne. 1993. *An Ethic of Care: Feminist and Interdisciplinary Perspectives*. New York: Routledge.

Levine, David. 1997. "Building Classroom Communities through Social Skills Development." *Educational Leadership* (October): 5–35.

Li, Xiaorong. 1998. "Asian Values and the Universality of Human Rights." *Business and Society Review* 102/103: 81–87.

Lickona, Thomas. 1980. "What Does Moral Psychology Have to Say to the Teacher of Ethics?" In *Ethics Teaching in Higher Education*, edited by Daniel Callahan and Sissela Bok, 103–132. New York: Plenum.

Luckowski, Jean A. 1997. "A Virtue-Centered Approach to Ethics Education." *Journal of Teacher Education* 48(4): 264–270.

Macintyre, Alasdair. 1997. "The Nature of Virtues." In *Virtue Ethics*, edited by Roger Crisp and Michael Slote. New York: Oxford University Press.

Macklin, Ruth. 1980. "Problems in the Teaching of Ethics: Pluralism and Indoctrination." In *Ethics Teaching in Higher Education*, edited by Daniel Callahan and Sissela Bok, 81–101. New York: Plenum.

McDowell, Banks. 1992. "The Ethical Obligations of Professional Teachers (of Ethics)." *Professional Ethics Journal* 1(3/4): 53–76.

Medicine, Beatrice. 2001. *Learning to Be an Anthropologist and Remaining Native*. Urban: University of Illinois Press.

Mill, John Stuart. 1991. *On Liberty and Other Essays*. Edited by John Gary. New York: Oxford University Press.

Momeyer, Richard W. 1980. "Teaching as a Moral Activity." *Teaching Philosophy* 3(2): 77–88.

———. 1995. "Teaching Ethics to Student Relativists." *Teaching Philosophy* 18(4): 21–31.

Moore, William S. 1994. "Student and Faculty Epistemology in the College Classroom: The Perry Scheme of Intellectual and Ethical Development." In (draft chapter) *Handbook of College Teaching: Theory and Applications*, edited by Keith Prichard and R. McLaran Sawyer. Westport, CT: Greenwood.

Mysak, Sonia. 1997. "Strategies for Promoting Ethical Decision-Making." *Journal of Gerontological Nursing* (January): 25–31.

Nash, Laura L. 1981. "Ethics without the Sermon." *Harvard Business Review* (November/December): 79–89.

Nicholson, Linda J. 1983. "Women, Morality, and History." *Social Research* 50: 514–536.

Noddings, Nel. 1984. *Caring: A Feminine Approach to Ethics and Moral Education*. Berkeley: University of California Press.

Norman, Richard. 2000. "Applied Ethics: What Is Applied to What?" *Utilitas* 12(2): 119–136.

Okin, Susan Moller. 1987. *Justice, Gender, and the Family*. New York: Basic.

Paden, Roger. 1987. "The Student Relativist as Philosopher." *Teaching Philosophy* 10(2): 15–19.

Parr, Susan Resneck. 1980. "The Teaching of Ethics in Undergraduate Nonethics Courses." *Liberal Education* 66(1): 51–66.

Parsons, Gerald M., and Bruce B. Johnson. 2001. "Does Teaching Ethics Make a Difference? A Preliminary Study Using an Outcomes Assessment Process." *NACTA Journal* (March): 51–57.

Pavela, Gary. 1999. "New Imperatives for Student Ethical Development," *Synfax Weekly Report*, June 14, 865–867.

Pederson, Carol, Laura Duckett, Geoffrey Maruyama, and Muriel Ryden. 1990. "Using Structured Controversy to Promote Ethical Decision Making." *Journal of Nursing Education* 29(4): 150–157.

Pelton, Lou, Jhinuk Chowdhury, and Scott Vitell. 1999. "A Framework for the Examination of Relational Ethics: An Interactionist Perspective." *Journal of Business Ethics* 19: 241–253.

Perry, Jr., William G. 1970. *Forms of Intellectual and Ethical Development in the College Years*. New York: Holt, Rinehart and Winston.

Perry Burney, G. D., and B. K. Takyi. 2002. "Self Esteem, Academic Achievement, and Moral Development among Adolescent Girls." *Journal of Human Behavior in the Social Environment* 5(2): 15–28.

Peterson, Nicolas, and Will Sanders. 1998. *Citizenship and Indigenous Australians: Changing Conceptions and Possibilities*. London: Cambridge University Press.

Phillips, D. Z. 1992. *Interventions in Ethics*. New York: State University of New York Press.

Pollock, Lansing. 1988. "Evaluating Moral Theories." *American Philosophical Quarterly* 25(3): 229–239.

Pritchard, Michael S. 1999. "Kohlbergian Contributions to Educational Programs for the Moral Development of Professionals." *Educational Psychology Review* 11(4): 395–409.

Puka, Bill. 1993. "The Liberation of Caring: A Different Voice for Gilligan's 'Different Voice.'" In *An Ethic of Care: Feminist and Interdisciplinary Perspectives*, edited by Carol Gilligan, 215–239. New York: Routledge.

Richards, Norvin. 1988. "Forgiveness." *Ethics* (October): 77–96.

Rorty, Amelie Oksenberg. 1993. "Moral Imperialism vs. Moral Conflict: Conflicting Aims of Education." In *Can Virtue Be Taught?* edited by Barbara Darling-Smith, 33–51. Notre Dame, IN: University of Notre Dame Press.

Rosen, Bernard. 1980. "The Teaching of Undergraduate Ethics." In *Ethics Teaching in Higher Education*, edited by Daniel Callahan and Sissela Bok, 171–189. New York: Plenum Press.

Rudolph, Lynn, and Linda Timm. 1998. "A Comprehensive Approach for Creating a Campus Climate that Promotes Academic Integrity." In *Academic Integrity Matters*, edited by Dana D. Burnett, Lynn Rudolph, and Karen Clifford. Washington, DC: National Association of Student Personnel Administrators.

Ruiz, Pedro Ortega, and Ramon Minguez Vallejos. 1999. "The Role of Compassion in Moral Education." *Journal of Moral Education* 28(1): 5–17.

Satris, Stephen A. 1986. "Student Relativism." *Teaching Philosophy* 9(3): 193–205.

Schott, Robin May. 1998. "Feminism and Kant: Antipathy or Sympathy?" In *Autonomy and Community: Readings in Contemporary Kantian Social Philosophy*, edited by Jane Kneller and Sidney Axinn, 229–249. New York: State University of New York Press.

Schrader, Dawn E. 1993. "Lawrence Kohlberg's Approach and the Moral Education of Educational Professionals." In *Ethics for Professionals in Education: Perspectives for Preparation and Practice*, edited by Kenneth A. Strike and P. Lance Ternasky, 84–101. New York: Teachers College Press.

Sedgwick, Sally. 1997. "Can Kant's Ethics Survive the Feminist Critique?" In *Feminist Interpretations of Immanuel Kant*, edited by Robin Schott, 77–100. May University Park: Pennsylvania State University Press.

Seifert, Josef. 1999. "Is Advocacy of Specific Philosophical Positions in the Classroom Pedagogically Acceptable?" *APA Newsletter on Teaching Philosophy* (Fall): 114–117.

Selby, Jane. 1999. "Cross-Cultural Research in Health Psychology." In *Qualitative Health Psychology: Theories and Methods*, edited by Michael Murray and Kerry Chamberlain, 164–180. London: Sage.

———. 2000. *Relationships of Impossibility: Professional Colonisers*. Bathurst, NSW, Australia: Centre for Cultural Research into Risk, Charles Sturt University.

———. 2003. "Discomfort in Research: Theorising from Dynamics across Indigenous Settings." In *Theoretical Advances in Psychology*, edited by N. Stephenson, H. L. Radtke, R. J. Jorna, and J. J. Stam, 358–367. Amsterdam: Kluwer.

———. 2004. "Disruptions of Identity: Dynamics of Working across Indigenous Differences." *Qualitative Studies in Education* 17(1): 143–156.

Sherman, Nancy. 1991. *The Fabric of Character: Aristotle's Theory of Virtue*. New York: Oxford University Press.

Shulman, B. 2002. "Is There Enough Poison Gas to Kill the City? The Teaching of Ethics in Mathematics Classes." *College Mathematics Journal* 33(2): 118–125.

Sichel, Betty A. 1992. "The Humanities and an Ethics of Care." In *Moral Education and the Liberal Arts*, edited by Michael H. Mitias, 125–145. New York: Greenwood.

Singer, Peter. 1995. *How Are We to Live? Ethics in an Age of Self-Interest*. New York: Prometheus.

Slote, Michael. 1997. "Agent-Based Virtue Ethics." In *Virtue Ethics*, edited by Roger Crisp and Michael Slote, 239–262. New York: Oxford University Press.

Smith, Huston. 1993. "Educating the Intellect: On Opening the Eye and the Heart." In *Can Virtue Be Taught?* edited by Barbara Darling-Smith, 17–31. Notre Dame, IN: University of Notre Dame Press.

Stern, Judy E., and Deni Elliott. 1997. *The Ethics of Scientific Research: A Guidebook for Course Development*. Hanover, NH: University Press of New England.

Superson, Anita M. 1999. "Sexism in the Classroom: The Role of Gender Stereotypes in the Evaluation of Female Faculty." *APA Newsletter on Feminism and Philosophy* (Fall): 46–51.

Tappan, Mark B. 2000. "Power, Privilege, and Critique in the Study of Moral Development." *Human Development* 43: 165–169.

Thoma, Stephen, J. 2000. "Models of Moral Development." *Journal of Mind and Behavior* 21(1/2): 129–136.

Tong, Rosemarie. 1993. *Feminine and Feminist Ethics*. Belmont, CA: Wadsworth.

Toulmin, Stephen. 1988. "The Recovery of Practical Philosophy." *American Scholar* 57(3): 337–352.

Wellman, Carl. 1972. "Ethics Since 1950." *Journal of Value Inquiry* VI(2): 83–90.

Whitbeck, Caroline. 1992. "The Trouble with Dilemmas: Rethinking Applied Ethics." *Professional Ethics* 1(1/2): 119–142.

White, H. Allen, and Charles R. Pearce. 1991. "Validating an Ethical Motivations Scale: Convergence and Predictive Ability." *Journalism Quarterly* 68(3): 455–464.

White, Steven H., and Joseph E. O'Brien. 1999. "What Is a Hero? An Exploratory Study of Students' Conceptions of Heroes." *Journal of Moral Education* 28(1): 81–95.

Whitman, Jeffrey P. 1998. "Exploring Moral Character in Philosophy Class." *Teaching Philosophy* 21(2): 171–182.

Wolf, Susan. 1982. "Moral Saints." *Journal of Philosophy* 79: 419–439.

Wolff, Robert Paul. 1969. "The Myth of the Neutral University." In *The Ideal of the University*, 103–109. Boston: Beacon.

Yazzie, Robert. 2002. "Bring Peacemakers into Courtrooms." *Utne Reader* (March/April): 55.

Zeuschner, Robert B. 2001. *Classical Ethics: East and West*. Boston: McGraw-Hill.

Index

About the Author

Deni Elliott holds the Poynter Jamison Chair in Media Ethics and Press Policy and is a professor in the Department of Journalism and Media Studies at the University of South Florida, St. Petersburg. She served as founding director for the Practical Ethics Center, was a professor in the Department of Philosophy at the University of Montana, and served as founding director for the Ethics Institute at Dartmouth College. Dr. Elliott also serves as the Ethics Officer for the Metropolitan Water District of Southern California. Her upcoming books include *An Involuntary Adventure*, which documents her experience with breast cancer and the questions it raises for ethical medical practice, and *On the Edge*, an irreverent look at unusual animal-human relationships.